APOLOGIES

to the

GRANDCHILDREN

Also by William Ophuls

Ecology an• the Politics of Scarcity
Requiem for Mo•ern Politics
Plato's Revenge: Politics in the Age of Ecology
Immo•erate Greatness: Why Civilizations Fail
Sane Polity: A Pattern Language

APOLOGIES

to the

GRANDCHILDREN

*Reflections on Our Ecological Predicament,
Its Deeper Causes, and Its Political Consequences*

WILLIAM OPHULS

ISBN: 9781730887253
Independently published

CONTENTS

THE

ECOLOGICAL

PREDICAMENT

1.

APOLOGIES TO THE GRANDCHILDREN

———————

Civilization is, by its very nature, a long-running Ponzi scheme. It lives by robbing nature and borrowing from the future, exploiting its hinterland until there is nothing left to exploit, after which it implodes. While it still lives, it generates a temporary and fictitious surplus that it uses to enrich and empower the few and to dispossess and dominate the many. Industrial civilization is the apotheosis and quintessence of this fatal course. A fortunate minority gains luxuries and freedoms galore, but only by slaughtering, poisoning, and exhausting creation. So we bequeath you a ruined planet that dooms you to a hardscrabble existence, or perhaps none at all.

I

It is not as though we did not have ample warning that industrial civilization was becoming the author of its own demise[1].

———————

1 What follows is not a complete record of ecological warnings. It leaves out many prominent names—for example, Paul Ehrlich, Garrett Hardin, and Herman Daly—because I have chosen to highlight reports of scientific consensus over individual works. I also focus more on overshoot and collapse rather than particular problems, like overpopulation.

In 1954 Harrison Brown argued that a profligate "machine civilization" was burning through resources at such a rate that it would soon be bankrupt[2]. Hence the industrial age was likely to be only a brief historical interlude between two long epochs of agrarian civilization. In the unlikely event that we escaped this fate, the outcome would be a nightmarishly regimented dystopia. He therefore urged humanity to make a timely transition to a high-level agrarian civilization, one that retained many technological advantages and offered the prospect of reasonably good life for centuries to come. To wait until necessity forced our hand would guarantee a bleak future of exhausted mines, depleted soils, toxic environments, and limited possibilities.

Brown's larger point was that political, social, and economic systems are decisively shaped by the quantity and quality of the available resources, especially the energy resources that are the sine qua non for exploiting every other resource. This was spelled out in more detail by Fred Cottrell in 1955. Using an array of historical examples, he showed that the availability of energy effectively determined the nature and fate of societies. And as the resource base on which it depended deteriorated, industrial civilization would experience a decline in the "net amount of surplus energy."[3] This would compel a painful re-

---

2 See List of Sources for works cited in the text.
3 Now known as EROI or EROEI (energy return on energy invested).

gression to the mean that existed before the age of fossil fuels—
i.e., an agrarian civilization.

Along these same lines, I argued in 1977 that the relatively open, egalitarian, individualistic, and libertarian societies prevailing in the modern world were the luxuriant fruit of
an era of unparalleled ecological abundance occasioned first by
Europe's appropriation of the New World's mostly untapped
resources and then by the exploitation of first coal and then
petroleum. The return of ecological scarcity presaged by the
decline in net energy, the depletion of major resources, the rise
in management costs, the growth in pollution, and the increase
in population would cause the process to operate in reverse.
The golden age of individualism, liberty, democracy, and mass
consumption would be over, and society would resume its former shape—namely, that of pre-industrial civilization, socially,
economically, and politically[4].

Industrialization and pollution have always gone hand-in-
hand but without diminishing the belief in economic growth
as an almost unmitigated good. That began to change in 1962
when Rachel Carson documented the harm caused by pes-

---

4 A recent work by Ian Morris explores in some detail how values, practices, and institutions are ruthlessly shaped by cultural selection for what works best given the quantity
and quality of energy available to a population. (Thus the radical differences in the lives of
foragers, farmers, and industrial peoples.) This evolutionary dynamic operates over time to
push societies at the same energy level toward a common structure with similar mores and
politics.

ticides, especially DDT, and by extension the danger of other organically active compounds released into the environment with little regard for ecological or human costs. And in 1965 the terrible consequences of heavy-metal poisoning from industrial pollution became apparent when heart-rending photos of the victims of Minamata Disease were widely published. The growing contamination of rivers and lakes with a variety of chemicals as well as of air sheds with smog also became headline news at this time. The result was some effort by the early 1970s to control the most glaring forms of pollution, but the steady drip of contaminants into the environment has never ceased, because it is intrinsic to mass consumption and the industrial process.

In 1972 the Club of Rome's report on the limits to growth expressed a deeper systemic understanding of humanity's ecological predicament. Donella Meadows and her colleagues constructed a simple but elegant computer model that linked data on food, population, pollution, industrial output, and resources to show their interaction over time. The model revealed that, if current trends were allowed to run their course, industrial civilization would overshoot by far the carrying capacity of the earth and experience a traumatic collapse. The authors suggested an array of reasonable policies to forestall this outcome. The report drew widespread attention, but also savage criticism (much of it uninformed), and its recommendations were not adopted. Other authors—myself in 1977 and William Catton in 1980—used prose to describe the same predicament: overshoot followed inevitably by collapse unless major remedial actions were taken decisively and soon.

Meanwhile, philosophical critics of industrial civilization saw its ecological sins as symptoms of a larger problem. In 1973 E. F. Schumacher argued that not only was modern technology unnecessarily harmful ecologically but also that it was mostly unnecessary, because we could make a reasonably good life for ourselves without depriving posterity if we were to use simpler, thriftier "intermediate technologies" more adapted to human needs. Then in a series of provocative works published from 1971 to 1974, Ivan Illich launched an attack on the values and practices of industrial civilization. He argued that the "shadow price" attached to industrial goods and services exceeded their true value, that industrial systems robbed individuals of agency and autonomy by exercising a radical monopoly over most spheres of life, and that as a consequence we had become inmates in a technological asylum. In effect, we were enslaved by our energy slaves and needed to free ourselves by slowing down and radically simplifying our lives.

More than a decade later, in 1990, the Intergovernmental Panel on Climate Change, a world-wide coalition of experts under the aegis of the United Nations, published the first in a series of reports documenting how human activities were inducing a slow but sustained warming of the atmosphere that, if allowed to continue, would have serious impacts on the biosphere and human life. Each successive report (the latest in 2013) has shown the evidence for human-caused climate change to be stronger and the urgency of action greater.[5] Because of inertia in the climate system, the impact of CO_2 on the atmosphere can take decades to manifest fully, making a proactive response essential. Although the international community has acted to curb emissions, the proposed measures appear to be too little and too late to prevent serious harm to the biosphere and human life.

An update to the Club of Rome's report appeared in 1992. It responded to valid criticisms of the original model and used newer data, but the outcome did not change. Except now that another 20 years had elapsed, the actions required to avoid the worst consequences of overshoot were both more stringent and

5   A more recent report issued by the U.S. government freshens the data and reaches a similar conclusion: the problem is very real and time grows ever shorter. See **USGCRP,** 2017: *Climate Science Special Report: Fourth National Climate Assessment, Volume I* [Wuebbles, D.J., D.W. Fahey, K.A. Hibbard, D.J. Dokken, B.C. Stewart, and T.K. Maycock (eds.)]. U.S. Global Change Research Program, Washington, DC, USA, 470 pp. See also the latest from the IPCC at www.ipcc.ch/report/sr15/

more urgent. The report attracted none of the attention of the original.

In that same year, 1,700 of the world's leading scientists published *Worl• Scientists' Warning to Humanity*. It said that human beings and the natural world were on a collision course that portended serious risks to both parties and urged fundamental changes to forestall catastrophe. In effect, it threw the full weight of the scientific establishment behind the ecological case for radical changes in our way of life. The response to this warning was business as usual.

Undeterred by the tepid reception of the 20-year update, the authors published a 30-year update of *Limits to Growth* in 2004. Refinements to the model and newer data changed almost nothing. In fact, the original model had tracked real-world trajectories very closely. However, an additional 10 years without decisive action to forestall overshoot and collapse had increased both the urgency and the magnitude of the required measures. Now only drastic actions would suffice. Again, the report attracted none of the attention of the original.

Then in 2017, 25 years after the original warning, 15,364 scientists from 184 countries signed *Worl• Scientists' Warning to Humanity: A Secon• Notice*. It's message was blunt: industrial civilization was courting catastrophe and needed a total makeover. Virtually all of the adverse trends specified in the first warning have worsened, and time has grown far shorter. Urgent and radical action was therefore needed to forestall widespread ecological damage and human misery.

Since the 13 actions specified in this second warning would stop industrial civilization in its tracks, cause massive disruption to business as usual, and require almost everyone to make major sacrifices, the likelihood of their being implemented, in whole or even in part, is effectively zero. As Illich warned, industrial man has become a slave to his energy slaves, totally addicted to the industrial production of goods and services and unable to envision any other way of life.

Illich also correctly intuited that the bads created by industrial civilization had begun to outweigh the goods. This is due to the operation of a basic physical law, the Entropy Law, which states that greater order (i.e., a good) in one part of a system inevitably implies greater disorder (i.e., a bad) in another. Thus when coal is burned in a power plant, only about 35 or 40 percent of the original energy in the coal becomes electricity (the good) while the remainder becomes pollution in one form or another (the bad), and even the good is dissipated as low-grade heat once it has done its work. To speak of fossil fuel use more generally, besides being a depleting, non-renewable resource, it necessarily involves a host of "negative externalities," "unintended consequences," and "side effects"—mostly euphemisms for bads, both ecological and social. Above all, it involves the release into the atmosphere of the CO_2 that causes the warming that will in turn lead to a rise in sea levels, desertification, extreme weather, and other threats to our current way of life.

Even areas not directly tied to energy production follow the same law. Modern medicine, for example, can perform what would have been seen as miracles in olden times, but the costs are high—not just financially, but also in terms of iatrogenic disease and other "side effects," such as the release of antibiotics and hormones into the environment where they have begun to negatively impact not only animal populations but also human health. The essential meaning of entropy for human life was well stated by Carl Jung: "Everything better is purchased at the price of something worse."[6]

If every good implies an equal and opposite bad—in fact, as the example of coal above illustrates, the bad can outweigh the good—what allowed the Industrial Revolution to be such a success? The answer is sixfold. First, most obvious, it began with an abundance of high-grade resources. Second, the original bads, such as industrial waste, were relatively small compared to the atmosphere or the rivers into which they were discharged. The harm did not go unnoticed, but the damage seemed minor compared to the benefits. Third, the benefits and costs of in-

---

6 *Memories, Dreams, Reflections*, 236.

dustrialization were not distributed equally. The industrialists and their allies profited greatly, the natural world and the poor, disadvantaged, or colonized paid the price. Fourth, due to inertia in the system, a major portion of the costs of industrialization were shoved into the future. As with the climate regime, the effect of current industrial activity does not always become apparent until decades later. Hence grandchildren pay for the ecological sins of grandparents. Fifth, even the slowest rate of growth is exponential. Thus the absolute amount of both goods and bads grows steadily over time, doubling and doubling again until the burden of bads becomes impossible to sustain. Finally, sixth, economic growth involves an inescapable increase in complexity whose management requires ever more time, energy, resources, and money—a burden that, again, grows larger over time, forcing the society to run harder and harder just to stay in the same place.

That industrial civilization is being strangled by a slowly tightening noose of ecological scarcity has been apparent to anyone who cares to examine the evidence without prejudice. Sadly, this patent reality continues to be mostly denied in societies made up largely of the passively uninformed and the passionately misinformed. But the fact is that humanity's current ecological footprint is roughly 60 percent more than the earth can sustain over the long term, and it continues to grow.[7] And the last several decades of less-than-robust economic growth have required a constantly increasing debt load along with widespread financial chicanery. This has kept the game going for a little longer, but only by further enriching the very apex of the wealth pyramid while condemning the middle to stagnation and the bottom to penury. So we have every indication that we are living on borrowed money and time. Unfortunately, rational behavior is not characteristic of addicts and ignoramuses, so the warning signs of overshoot are denied or rationalized away by a divided, distracted, and deluded populace, and this would not change even if 100 percent of the world's scientists were to issue a warning to humanity. So far from trying to solve our problems, we persist in the behavior that makes them worse.

This state of affairs cannot continue. System theorists warn that although overshoot develops gradually, collapse tends to happen rapidly and often suddenly. And the pace of ecological deterioration has indeed accelerated. Whether it is the impact of a warming climate on polar ice, the decimation of fish stocks and the acidification of oceans, the rapid decline of insect and bird populations (not to mention the increased rate of extinction in general), the growing loss of topsoil due to industrial

---

7   See www.footprintnetwork.org

agriculture,[8] or the various ways in which chronic, low-grade pollution has begun to impact animal and human health, the evidence is mounting across the board that the ecosystems on which we depend are unraveling and that we may be approaching thresholds leading to irreversible changes. To be specific, we risk entering a regime of positive feedback producing runaway change, as when global warming threatens to unlock the CO_2 and methane now sequestered in permafrost.

Given the accelerating trend toward ecological scarcity, humanity can no longer postpone adaptation to the end of the fossil-fuel era. Barging ahead with business as usual will relatively soon trigger a collapse—perhaps gradual and shallow, but more likely rapid and deep. Even if we avoid oblivion, the result would be a dark age whose darkness would be roughly proportional to the extent of the overshoot. To avoid such a fate, humanity must either achieve a total technological mastery over nature via the perfection of artificial intelligence and robotics, an outcome that has been dubbed the Singularity, or make a rel-

---

8 At the current rate of depletion, the world's topsoil will be effectively gone in six decades. Chris Arsenault, "Only 60 Years of Farming Left If Soil Degradation Continues," Scientific American/Reuters accessed at https://www.scientificamerican.com/article/only-60-years-of-farming-left-if-soil-degradation-continues/ See also, World Economic Forum, "What If the World's Soil Runs Out?," *Time*, December 14, 2012.

atively fast transition to a high-level agrarian civilization, precisely the options posited many years ago by Harrison Brown.

In reality, however, a state of total technological mastery is probably not achievable owing to basic physical and biological laws, such as the Entropy Law and the Law of the Minimum. Technology cannot sustain a "machine civilization" or even a "digital civilization" out of thin air.[9] In addition, as noted by Brown, the Singularity would be a regimented, collectivized dystopia. (The digital panopticon of today is but the merest harbinger of such a future.) Humanity might survive, but it would no longer be recognizably human. Aiming for the Singularity would also be the kind of high-risk gamble that wise strategists abhor. For if we should fail in the attempt to achieve it, we will have used up all our remaining resources in a lost cause, thus guaranteeing a deep collapse into the darkest of dark ages, if not oblivion.

So here is where we stand. We are hurtling toward a day of ecological reckoning. We should have acted many years ago to contain the damage and build a bridge to a different kind of civilization. Now we are faced with an increased population, worse pollution, dwindling resources, progressive biological destruction, much greater complexity, compounding debt, and

---

9 See Kris De Decker, "The Monster Footprint of Digital Technology," *Low-Tech Magazine*, June 16, 2009. Accessed at http://www.lowtechmagazine.com/2009/06/embodied-energy-of-digital-technology.html. This footprint is growing rapidly. See https://arstechnica.com/tech-policy/2017/12/bitcoins-insane-energy-consumption-explained/

enormous inertia in the system—a nexus of problems that have no separate solutions, only an aggregate solution requiring a total revolution in our way of life.

II

If we were wise, or had any concern for or posterity, we would now confront ecological reality and make a virtue out of necessity by transitioning as soon as possible to an agrarian society while we still have the wherewithal to create a relatively prosperous and egalitarian political economy, instead of one marked by scarcity and duress.[10] Alas, we are not wise, or even very smart, but merely clever. So we will continue poisoning and impoverishing the earth until we blunder into a terminal crisis.

In an ideal world, government at every level would be making plans for the great simplification to come. As generals have learned, even the best war plans rarely survive first contact with the enemy, but having planned is essential, because it forces you to imagine different scenarios and to prepare for the worst. In other words, planning is an inoculation against stupefaction and panic, so when things do not go according to plan, you are less likely to lose your head and quicker to make

---

10 In reality, nothing is more difficult than to reform a civilization. Making changes to a poorly understood complex adaptive system can precipitate the collapse you are trying to avoid. But when in extremis, as we are or soon will be, there is no choice but to make the attempt.

the necessary adjustments.[11] But this is not an ideal world. To the extent that governments are seriously looking ahead to a future beyond the electoral cycle, they are doing their level best to preserve industrial civilization in more or less its current form, not to replace it with something different. When that effort fails and industrial civilization begins to break down, stupefaction and panic are probably what we will get.

Our descent into chaos and turmoil will precipitate a struggle for survival for which we are totally unprepared, individually or collectively. As the manifestations of collapse multiply, the masses will be bewildered and angry, while the elites will be attempting to perform damage control with no real understanding of what to do, much less a vision of a desirable future that they want to create. It will be a severe test of character for both peoples and individuals. Many, if not most, will fail the test.

The outcome will be partly determined by how badly damaged and depleted the earth is when the terminal crisis strikes, partly by the degree to which the worst forms of madness can be avoided, and partly whether fate is kind to us. The outcome will also be different according to location. The most advanced economies are the most dependent on highly integrated systems of support that may not survive even a relatively shallow

---

11   See Appendix for how officials at all levels might be prepared for the consequences of breakdown.

collapse. It is one thing when disaster strikes and outside aid is available to provide relief and to help rebuild; it is quite another thing if everyone is in the same dire circumstances with nothing left but their own bootstraps. And even if there is some possibility of mutual aid after the crisis, rebooting the energy-dependent, complex systems we rely on today would be a herculean task even if we had an abundance of resources. Ronald Wright's metaphor is apt: as we climbed the ladder of "progress," we kicked out the rungs below, leaving us stranded and helpless with no graceful or practical way to climb down once disaster strikes. Paradoxically, therefore, those who are accustomed to a simple life without modern conveniences and who win their subsistence locally and directly from the earth may be better positioned not only to to survive the crisis but also to reconstruct their societies along the lines envisioned by Schumacher and Illich.

The upshot for individuals in "advanced" economies dependent on global systems rather than local resources for basic necessities is that they will be largely on their own. If they want to thrive, or even survive, our grandchildren will need to be like the tough, hard-working, cooperative, jacks and jills-of-all-trades that built industrial civilization in the first place. However, even more than technical skills and practical nous, the right mindset will be critical. Instead of hankering after a

restoration of a high mass-production and consumption society, they will need to look resolutely forward—aiming to create a civilization founded on radically different principles, one
that that is in harmony with biological and physical reality and
that relies for its sustenance on the annual flow of solar energy
instead of the stock of solar capital laid down in previous ages.

III

A first glance, it seems hardly possible to depict an attractive
future. Those in the more developed economies accustomed to
the luxury of flicking a switch or turning a key and having energy slaves instantly doing their bidding will undoubtedly recoil
at the prospect of doing without modern conveniences, not to
mention having to do much of the work that these slaves used
to do. And the world's poor will hardly welcome an end to their
own dreams of affluence. It is also evident that today's world
population of 7.6 billion is far too large to be supported by the
flow of solar energy, so a benign future depends upon a radical
reduction in numbers.[12] In addition, agrarian civilizations are
no paradise. As James Scott points out, the earliest city states
repeatedly collapsed when farmers—rebelling against disease,

---

12 It is not possible to state with certainty what a sustainable population level would be, but
back-of-the-envelope calculations suggest 1-2 billion. To attain this level in the reasonably
near future would not require a massive die off, although that may indeed occur, because a
mere 2 percent surplus of deaths over births per annum would achieve this level by the end
of the century.

toil, and oppression—deserted them to resume the more agreeable life of foraging.[13] It was only when the latter option was foreclosed by the relentless geographical advance of agriculture that agrarian civilization was able to put down roots and develop into the stable, complex societies that characterize antiquity.

However, we now know of alternatives that are both less backbreaking and potentially less oppressive than the extensive cultivation of cereal grains. (As Scott points out, this form of agriculture is inescapably marked not only by toil and disease but also by the predation of tax collectors and other vermin.) Paradoxically and sadly, many of the agricultural alternatives proposed by modern reformers, such as permaculture, were practiced by the pre-Columbian peoples of the Americas. Unfortunately, the conquest of the New World devastated its populations and virtually eradicated pre-existing ways of life. Hence these highly sophisticated agricultural practices were lost and are only now being rediscovered by anthropologists.[14] Putting this knowledge together with what we might be able to keep of modern technology means that we have material possibilities undreamt of by our ancestors. The question is, do we have the wit to employ them to make a timely and orderly transition to

---

13 See Suzman for why foraging can be more attractive than farming and what we can learn for our own future from our hunter-gatherer ancestors.

14 Charles C. Mann, "1491", *Atlantic Monthly*, March 2002. Access at https://www.theatlantic.com/magazine/archive/2002/03/1491/302445/

a technically and agriculturally sophisticated agrarian civilization?

More important is the question of political and social arrangements. And here we can offer the hope of a saner and
more humane post-industrial order. Jean-Jacques Rousseau
pinpointed the fundamental contradiction of a life devoted to
consumption by saying, "For the impulse of appetite alone is
slavery, and obedience to the law one has prescribed for oneself
is freedom."[15] In this light, moving away from our current state
of addiction to appetite would be a positive development, however deeply resisted at first, because it would allow us to create
a way of life that is both in harmony with nature and also in
accord with the deepest political and spiritual wisdom.

Although the quantity and quality of available energy indeed determines the fundamental shape of a society, the details
of agrarian social and political arrangements can vary enor-
mously. For instance, traditional Bali and Tokugawa Japan both
depended on rice cultivation but had very different aesthetic,
social, economic, and political cultures. And 18th century England, which relied on mixed farming, was very different from
both. But they all had a class structure—relatively relaxed in
Bali, quite strict in Japan and England—with the bulk of the
population attached to the soil at the bottom and much small-

---

15 *Social Contract*, I, viii. See also Illich, *Energy an⬩ Equity*, 6: "The energy crisis focuses
concern on the scarcity of fodder for these slaves. I prefer to ask if free men need them."

er strata of merchants, landlords, soldiers, officials, and rulers above. And they also had a moral structure—again, more re-laxed or quite strict depending on the culture—that imposed sanctions but that also supplied a framework of mores that united the society.[16]

So we have a wide latitude of choice within the limits set by the flow of solar energy. It is possible in principle to create an agricultural civilization founded on yeoman farmers instead of exploited peasants or slaves—that is, the kind of small-hold, egalitarian, salt-of-the-earth farming society that Thomas Jefferson envisioned for the United States. I have imagined such an agrarian civilization, which I call "Bali with electronics."[17] In short, we can have benign and culturally rich societies without energy slavery. True, these societies may not offer the kinds of permissive freedoms that many enjoy today; individuals will have to find their freedom within the prevailing moral frame-work, not apart from it. But in return they will get back the

16 See Azby Brown for a richly detailed portrait of life in Tokugawa Japan. Its political and social structure may not constitute a model we would want to emulate, but many of its values, practices, and techniques suggest the direction in which we will be compelled to move.
17 Ophuls, 2011, 179. See also the whole of Chap. 7, which advocates a political future based on ecological principles and the ideas of Rousseau, Jefferson, and Thoreau.

autonomy, agency, and integrity that were lost in societies given over to distraction and consumption.

The famous lines of Wordsworth point to the deeper spiritual issue:

Getting and spending, we lay waste our powers;—
Little we see in Nature that is ours;
We have given our hearts away, a sordid boon!

What profit is it to wallow in pleasure and permissiveness if it costs us our hearts? Would a panel of the wise—Confucius, Gautama Buddha, Jesus of Nazareth, Lao Tzu, Rumi, and Socrates—conceivably approve of our current way of life? Obviously not. What the impending ecological crisis forces us to confront is that we have sacrificed meaning, morality, and almost all higher values for the "sordid boon" of material wealth and worldly power. To keep drinking from this poisoned chalice will bring only sickness and death.

IV

The ecological challenge facing humanity has been compared to the Neolithic Revolution that established agrarian civilization in the first place. In fact, that "revolution" was a long, drawn-out affair lasting well over a thousand years, whereas we will soon be resuming this condition rather abruptly after a mere two and a half centuries of industrial existence. Thus a better analogy is the Mauryan Emperor Ashoka's conversion to Buddhism in the aftermath of a terrible war of conquest in which he was victorious but sickened by the cost of victory. What Ashoka experienced is called metanoia—a transformative change of heart, especially a spiritual conversion. And this is exactly what is required today: a profound transformation of consciousness that abjures self-destructiveness and selfishness, manifests a will to live in harmony with nature, and aspires to some higher values than worldly wealth and bodily comfort.

We live in a civilization that produces goods in abundance but not the Good. It is generally thought that the so-called death of God, after which everything is permitted, resulted in nihilism. While this is certainly true—who would deny that we have largely abandoned traditional morality?—it is only a part of the truth, and the lesser part at that. For industrial civilization does in fact have a tacit religion: the worship of Mammon, a false god that incites us to lay waste our powers in getting and spending.

So we bequeath you the monumental task of reestablishing civilization on principles that are sane, humane and ecological. And it is indeed up to you; your elders are probably irredeemable. While we may have left you with little in the way of resources, your task is not hopeless. In the end civilization is not something material, it is spiritual. Be inspired by the beauty of the cosmos to invent a way of being devoted to feeding the soul instead of filling the belly. Rediscover the spiritual abundance that resides in material simplicity. Learn again that the only wealth worth having lies in the treasury of the human heart.

> How simple and frugal a thing is happiness: a glass of wine, a roast chestnut, a wretched little brazier, the sound of the sea...All that is required...is a simple, frugal heart.[18]

---

18 Nikos Kazantzakis, *Zorba the Greek*, trans. Carl Wildman, (New York: Simon & Schuster, 1996), 80.

2.

WHAT CAN GIVE US HOPE?

Industrial civilization is in a hopeless position, an impasse from which there is no visible avenue of escape. It cannot continue moving forward for very much longer, because it is encountering multiple physical, biological, economic, and systemic limits to growth that are already having adverse spillover effects on polity and society, as well as on human health. Nor can industrial civilization stand still, because its political, economic, and social viability requires continuous growth. Above all, economic growth is indispensable psychologically, because "progress" defined as ever-increasing knowledge, wealth, and power has been the secular religion of modern civilization for over three centuries. Hence an end to growth would crush morale. (The impact would be especially severe in the United States, for it is the shared dream of unlimited freedom and universal prosperity embodied in the so-called American Dream—not America's vaunted, but increasingly dysfunctional, constitutional arrangements—that unites a nation divided by geography, ideology, interest, class, education, religion, race, and ethnicity.) Nor can we easily descend to a previous level of production and consumption, because we have almost obliterated the older skills and less complex technologies that would allow us to beat an orderly retreat to a simpler mode of existence. Ronald Wright's image neatly captures our plight: "As we climbed the ladder of progress, we kicked out the rungs below."[19]

Of course, not everyone sees the situation as hopeless. Some evince a touching faith in technology, blithely claiming without further elaboration that it will solve all of humanity's problems.[20] After all, it always has up to now, so why worry? Others make a more serious case for a technological solution. For some, renewable energy will seamlessly replace fossil fuels, solving the problem of depletion and pollution and allowing business as usual to continue for the foreseeable future. Others claim that exponential growth in artificial intelligence combined with robotics, nanotechnology, and other developments will lead to a state of technical and managerial perfection, to what has been called the Singularity. Both of these are false hopes.

Taking up the latter first, the Singularity appears not only to violate basic laws of physics and ecology—to wit, the Laws

---

19 *A Short History of Progress*, 34.

20 See, for example, "An Ecomodernist Manifesto." available at www.ecomodernism.org. The authors acknowledge particular ecological problems but ignore the general problem of overshoot and ecological footprint. They also rely on fusion and other unproven technologies to make their case.

of Thermodynamics and the Law of the Minimum—but it also seems to be more dystopia than utopia. For it would be a state in which humanity might continue to exist in some form but would be effectively eclipsed by the Machine.[21]

Renewable energy as a replacement for fossil fuels seems plausible at first glance, but it also turns out to be a false hope if it involves the belief that renewable energy will allow industrial civilization to continue more or less as it exists today. Some renewable sources (e.g., hydroelectric and geothermal) slot relatively easily into the current centralized energy system in that they can produce power continuously. But most do not: solar, wind, waves, and tides are diffuse and intermittent. If they are going to be our chief sources of electricity, then the infrastructure of our energy system will have to change accordingly—that is, be revolutionized at great expense by building local grids and storage systems adapted to power sources that are dispersed and discontinuous.[22] A primary reliance on renewable energy will also require a revolution in transportation, for without energy-dense liquid fuels derived from petroleum, economies will necessarily become far more local. The ships, trucks, and planes

---

21 See also "Is This the End of the Human Race?"

22 The difficulties, dangers, expense, and security issues associated with nuclear power are a topic for another time. Suffice it to say that it has not lived up to the promise of "electricity too cheap to meter," and even its proponents concede that it needs to be made safer and cheaper. Nor is nuclear power a source of *renewable* energy. Fusion power may eventually be demonstrated in laboratories, but it seems very unlikely to scale up in a way that is cost effective, either energetically or financially.

that bring bottled water from the antipodes and allow us to vacation in the Antipodes will not run on electricity.[23] In theory, biofuel could partially substitute for fossil fuel, but only at the expense of the crops that supply us with food and fiber, crops that are now almost completely dependent on the energy subsidy supplied by petroleum. Without this subsidy, which electricity cannot realistically replace, we will be hard pressed to feed anything like the current population, much less produce any substantial quantity of biofuel. Hydrogen is a possible liquid fuel, but it first has to be manufactured and then liquified, stored, transported, and delivered, all of which demand sophisticated technology and a complex infrastructure. Whether it proves to be both practicable and profitable (in energetic terms) remains to be seen. Finally, to build out an energy system based on renewable sources will require massive amounts of up-front capital and, more important, much of the remaining, rapidly depleting stocks of fossil fuel—and the more extensive the build out, the more subject to diminishing returns. Hence, when all is said and done, this colossal investment in diffuse renewable energy, so different from concentrated fossil fuels, would fall

---

23 I am not arguing that there are no technological solutions whatsoever. For example, short-distance air travel with electric power is certainly feasible. Whether it proves to be efficient and economical remains undetermined, and for short or even medium distances trains would seem to be just as convenient and more cost effective. Moreover, to the extent that we do substitute electricity for liquid fuel the demand on the grid will be that much greater.

well short of what is required to support the complex industrial civilization of today.[24]

So humanity would be going all in on a bet that we can preserve industrial civilization in its current form, when the essential nature of renewable energy mandates a more simple, decentralized way of life—viz., a smaller population spread more widely across the land relying mostly on the daily flow of solar energy and consuming goods and services produced locally. In short, an agrarian civilization, however well endowed with sophisticated technologies unavailable to previous civilizations that relied on direct solar energy. True, such a life would not be luxurious. We would have to adapt ourselves once again to the daily and seasonal rhythms of nature instead of commanding her with energy slaves—for example, by substituting sophisti-

---

24 For more detail on why renewable energy cannot support our current industrial order, see Kris De Decker, "How (Not) to Run a Modern Society on Wind and Solar Power Alone," September 14, 2017 retrieved at http://www.resilience.org/stories/2017-09-14/how-not-to-run-a-modern-society-on-solar-and-wind-power-alone/ And for an in-depth explanation of why renewable energy requires a total system change, see Richard Heinberg and David Fridley, *Our Renewable Future* (Washington, DC: Island Press, 2016).

cated sailing ships for motor vessels. But it need not be penurious provided we aim for it now.[25]

We face a stark choice. We can expend our waning stocks of fossil fuels, our scarce capital, and our limited political will in a vain attempt to maintain industrial civilization as it exists, or we can use those same resources to effect a necessary transition to a radically different type of civilization. But we cannot do both, and we must choose reasonably soon. For if we follow the line of least political and societal resistance and wager everything on an attempt to preserve our energy-intensive, mass-consumptive way of life, we will go bankrupt energetically. Without the resources to make the transition, deep collapse will become inescapable.

Alas, we seem almost compelled to make the wager. It is abundantly clear that scientific evidence and rational arguments, no matter how weighty or well formulated, are not enough to overcome sheer inertia, vested interests, ideological blinders, the shortcomings of the human mind, or the extent to which we are all increasingly entangled in the trappings of modern life.[26] Thus industrial civilization seems destined to

25 For a description of how such a renewable society might operate, see Kris De Decker, "How to Run the Economy on the Weather," September 25, 2017, retrieved at http://www.resilience.org/stories/2017-09-25/how-to-run-the-economy-on-the-weather/. See also Ophuls and Boyan, *Ecology an• the Politics of Scarcity Revisite•*, Box 14 "The Multiplex Energy Economy of the Future," 120-121.

26 Even the Amish have taken to smartphones! "In Amish Country, the Future Is Calling," *New York Times*, Sept. 15, 2017.

continue on its current trajectory until one or more of the limits bites so deeply as to precipitate collapse.

As industrial civilization begins to implode, we will witness an upsurge of prophecy of all kinds—fantastic, salvational, millenarian, apocalyptic, and reactionary. The aforementioned Singularity, a prophecy of salvation through technology, is one early example. But as a preview of coming attractions in a similar vein, consider one Silicon Valley engineer's proposal for a new religion: "To develop and promote the realization of a Godhead based on artificial intelligence and through understanding and worship of the Godhead contribute to the betterment of society."[27]

However, reaction will probably be more common than salvation. We can expect the emergence of revitalization movements exalting old-time customs, values, and verities and seeking a return to some prior state of purity or perfection.[28] Such movements can take various forms—messianic cults, tribal or racial extremism, religious fundamentalism, political rebellion, and so forth. At best, revitalization manifests a stubborn refusal to make a reasonable accommodation to a changed reality; at worst, it can become a violent attempt to change that real-

27 "Deus ex machina: former Google engineer is developing an AI god," *The Guardian*, September 28, 2017.

28 A classic example is the Ghost Dance promulgated by the Paiute prophet Wovoka. See also "The Perfect Storm."

ity. Although revitalization is fated to grow worse as conditions deteriorate, it is already a significant political force. A veteran observer of world affairs spells out the contents of the "violent reactionary current" of today:

> It is a rightist, nativist, nationalist...reaction against globalization, against migration, against miscegenation, against the disappearance of borders and the blurring of genders, against the half-tones of political correctness, against Babel, against the stranger and the other, against the smug self-interested consensus of the urban, global elite.[29]

Virtually all of these movements will fail more or less spectacularly. But the prophetic madness attending the death throes of industrial civilization will also contain a small but significant ray of hope: out of the welter of false prophets there may arise one whose message will effect the metanoia that is the only real way out of the impasse. For only by transcending our obsession with material power and progress and recovering a deep empathic connection to the planet and the life it bears can we hope to reconstruct civilization to be sane, humane, and ecological.

---

29 Roger Cohen, "Return of the German Volk," *New York Times*, September 29, 2017.

THE DEMISE OF

LIBERAL

DEMOCRACY

3.

PROLOGUE

Take but degree away, untune that string,
And, hark, what discord follows! each thing meets
In mere oppugnancy. . . . .
Force should be right; or rather, right and wrong,
Between whose endless jar justice resides,
Should lose their names, and so should justice too.
Then every thing includes itself in power,
Power into will, will into appetite;
And appetite, an universal wolf,
So doubly seconded with will and power,
Must make perforce an universal prey,
And last eat up himself.
— William Shakespeare, *Troilus an• Cressi•a*, I, iii

Shakespeare was an astute student of politics. His histories, which are explicitly political, constitute a third of his oeuvre, and most of his tragedies, which constitute another third, are also vitally concerned with politics. To read the word *•egree—* an archaic usage denoting social or official rank—as referring only to the aristocratic society of his time would therefore be a mistake. Shakespeare's core meaning is that there must be an orderly society—characterized by a certain ranking of persons, classes, values, and mores—or anarchy and violence are sure to follow.

John Locke, the foundational philosopher of modern politics, called this orderly structure "civil society," and he made it the indispensable framework for containing the disparate and sometimes opposing elements of societies no longer subject to the divine right of kings. Such societies are characterized by a tension between liberalism and conservatism. Unfortunately, these words have now been so bastardized in common use that it may take some effort to recover their original meanings, so that we can understand what has become of them and what that implies for our future.

The original liberals and conservatives both espoused the basic principles of liberal-democratic societies rooted in the ideas of Locke and others—in other words, the critical necessity of a functioning civil society—but they differed in one crucial respect. Conservatives valued order and conformity over the urge for personal freedom, but not to the detriment of individual liberty. Liberals valued personal freedom over the urge for order and conformity, but not to the detriment of social stability. Thus the good society was one in which the liberal-con-

servative tension was balanced: enough liberty along with sufficient stability. To put it another way, traditional liberals and
conservatives both understood that a well-ordered civil society
was essential, for without it there could be neither liberty nor
stability. To borrow the words of Yeats, when the center does
not hold, mere anarchy is loosed upon the world.

Unfortunately, that is the direction in which we are headed, for those who call themselves liberals and conservatives today have effectively abandoned civil society. On the left, liberals
largely devote themselves to asserting the rights of ever tinier
minorities and demanding that the "dominant culture"—that is,
what remains of civil society—change to accommodate those
who refuse to follow traditional norms.[30] And for the most part,
they been successful in converting the younger generation to
embrace this antinomian stance.

The situation is more complicated on the conservative
side. One very large group, composed of those left behind by
economic changes or alienated by social changes, circles the
wagons and withdraws consent. As President Obama said in an
unguarded moment, "They get bitter, they cling to guns or religion or antipathy to people who aren't like them or anti-immi-
grant sentiment or anti-trade sentiment." The rest fancy them-

---

30   This explosion of rights assertion is likely to be seen by historians as a sunset effect—i.e.,
the ultimate expression of personal freedom just as the ecological basis for individual liberty
is about to disappear.

selves masters of the universe after the fashion of Ayn Rand; they are "sovereign individuals" who owe nothing to the society that raised them and that continues to provide the structure of laws and institutions underlying their success. So they too withdraw consent and reject the constraints and obligations of civil society.

This increasingly polarized and divided society is reflected in the media, where the extremes, fringes, and outliers consume whatever space is left by the frenetic antics of politicians. Thus the *New York Times* expends its editorial might promoting transgender rights, the concern of a tiny minority, while Fox News rants in opposition to them. So climate change and other vital concerns for the society as a whole get pushed to the media margins. Pundits occasionally lament this fact, but to little effect.

There is no solution to this state of affairs. Once a social order unravels, it cannot be reconstituted, just as the bound energy in a lump of coal vanishes once it has been burned. Societies too are subject to entropy: the original élan, morale, and morals of a society inevitably dissipate over time. Thus it takes a episode of extraordinary politics—usually involving turmoil, bloodshed, and suffering—to achieve a new political consensus as the basis for a new civil society.If we now consider the impending avalanche of crises broadly grouped under the umbrella of ecology—climate change, soil loss, deforestation, extinctions, water shortages, and the like—the grounds for optimism about the immediate future almost disappear. It would be miraculous for societies that are being pulled apart to suddenly begin to pull together to solve the existential challenge that confronts them. Thus the necessity to examine in depth the fatal flaws of liberal democracy allied to economic growth and then to envision the type of political economy that seems likely to succeed it once the coming episode of extraordinary politics has reached its terminus.

4.

THE PERFECT STORM

What is most astonishing about the surge of reaction sweeping much of the developed and even developing world is that we are astonished by it. How could we not have foreseen that the vast "disruption" unleashed by globalization, digitalization, automation, artificial intelligence, and migration would sooner or later produce a reactionary response? A cascade of change is challenging the limits of human adaptability, destroying the old order—to the profit of some, but to the detriment of many—and propelling us toward a new order that is more hierarchical, unequal, rigid, and conformist (see "The Shape of a Future Civilization"). This was bound to provoke widespread anguish and resistance. For although human beings enjoy novelty, they deeply fear change.

That people can be persuaded by factual or scientific arguments to change their minds is demonstrably false. Confirmation bias—we take in information that supports our existing beliefs and mostly ignore or reject the rest—is only one of the many tricks the human mind plays on itself. Hence we respond to new facts in less-than-rational and often sub-optimal ways.

Indeed, adding the findings of neuroscience, behavioral economics, and the like to depth psychology reveals us to be barely rational beings, prisoners of subconscious brain circuitry driven largely by primitive emotion. Per Thomas Kuhn, scientists are not fully rational even within their own domain, and outside of it they are just as deluded as the rest of us—in some cases more so, precisely because they believe so firmly in their own rationality. Nor are the so-called best and brightest exempt. Far from it, said historian Barbara Tuchman: "Inertia in the scales of history weighs more heavily than change,"[31] and statesmen often pursue disastrous policies because they are "woodenheaded" and prone to "folly."[32] In the end, it could be said of most human beings that they have a large wooden block in their heads—an emotional-intellectual attachment to the reigning paradigm and the conventional wisdom—that can only be dislodged by main force.

Change can be unwelcome or challenging even when there is no particular reason to fear its consequences. But if it threatens stability, order, or an established way of life, then fear, anger, and hatred can become epidemic. Aversion to even trivial losses is another well demonstrated trait of the human mind; how much more so if one's entire way of life is threatened. Many will abandon reason altogether, denying the unde-

---

31 *A Distant Mirror*, 397.

32 *The March of Folly.*

niable, accepting lies as truth, ignoring blatant contradictions, and believing in impossibilities. (The current stupefaction of the mainstream media in the face of such irrationality would be a comedy if it were not a tragedy.)

To put it another way, the initial response to an existential threat to the established order will usually be what anthropologists call "revitalization": a fanatical reaffirmation of tradition rather than a reasonable accommodation to the new reality. Thus the Paiute and other Western tribes tried to counter the threat to their existence with a Ghost Dance that they fervently believed would repulse the white invaders and allow them to resume their habitual way of life. The world is now experiencing something similar: those who have been disadvantaged by disruption are demanding the restoration of a vanishing status quo ante. The old order may not have been paradise, but it was at least comfortable and known. Like the original Ghost Dance, this irrational attempt to ward off unwelcome but inescapable change is doomed to failure.

An upsurge of irrationality is a mortal threat to democratic polity. Political truth is always biased to some extent, but there is a profound and crucial difference between limited rationality and complete irrationality, relative objectivity and pure fantasy, demonstrable facts and blatant lies. A sane information environment is a precondition for a workable democracy. Once reality has been hijacked, there can be no reasonable basis for either voting or legislating.

To this we must add an even more ominous development— namely, the destruction of civil society caused by an excess of democracy. A well-functioning civil society is the indispensable container for the human passions. As Freud said, repression is the precondition for civilization. If society does not both set limits on the passions and provide avenues for their sublimation, then we must expect the return of the repressed in the form of widespread irrationality accompanied by noxious political consequences, as has been repeatedly demonstrated by history.

In particular, the breakdown of civil society is responsible for a resurfacing of tribalism, the latent tendency to see the world in terms of us against them (and therefore as zero-sum). And also for an inclination toward autocracy, a readiness to believe that some political genius will arise to solve all the vexing problems created by the bungling "elite." To speak in particular of the American polity, there have always been class, racial, and regional differences, but there was nevertheless a felt sense of belonging—of being in it together—that for the most part transcended these differences. No longer. Urban and rural, more educated and barely educated, coastal and interior are now different countries with little in common and mostly contrary values.

Lacking any sense of noblesse oblige, the cutting-edge coastal elite has gone its own way, confident that it is in the right—economically, socially, politically, morally—and if the "yokels" are not happy about it, so much the worse for them. It is only to be expected that the latter would one day react to being written out of the social contract and vote to overthrow the established order. As they have already had their way of life done in by the so-called elite, what do they have to lose?

The understanding that democracy in excess creates a chaos that invites tyranny goes back to Plato. In Book VIII of *The Republic*, Socrates describes what later came to be called the cycle of regimes. In essence, each type of political regime—for example, aristocracy, oligarchy, and democracy—is eventually undone by its flaws, creating the conditions for the next to arise, thrive for a time, and then be replaced in turn by a new one when its flaws come to dominate.[33] Thus when the freedom and equality that are the virtues and hallmarks of democracy go too far, the polity is split into fractions. Individuals increasingly go their own way, pursuing their own selfish ends and their separate identities and destinies. Gender roles break down. Established forms of authority are disregarded or attacked. Tra-

---

33 See my *Requiem for Modern Politics*. By abandoning virtue, rejecting community, and flouting nature, polities founded on Enlightenment principles have become the author of their own demise. The democratic breakdown, radical inequality, and ecological degradation evident today are the lawful and fated outcome of the individualism, hedonism, and rationalism fomented by the Enlightenment.

ditional morals go by the board; the word transgressive is spoken in praise. Voting is more and more driven by instinct and prejudice, not reason and interest. Those in charge expend all their energy in infighting, not governing. In short, the polity becomes increasingly dysfunctional, decadent, and delusional. Plato's portrait of democratic chaos—and of the would-be tyrant who offers salvation—seems ripped from today's newspapers.

Similar concerns were expressed in The *Federalist Papers*. Madison and the other framers of the American Constitution justified its undemocratic checks and balances as necessary to forestall the chaos that their reading of history showed followed inescapably in the wake of democracy. And although Alexis de Tocqueville acknowledged and even celebrated the virtues of American democracy, he also foresaw the emergence of authoritarianism once democracy's pernicious shadow side had undermined the foundation of those virtues. Indeed, all those who have thought seriously about democracy have generally agreed that it depends crucially on a certain set of conditions: a well functioning, stable civil society grounded on a shared history, language, and ethos, if not a common religion. Large, sprawling, diverse, polyglot societies are more demanding and complex to govern and have therefore traditionally been ruled as empires, with democracy confined to homogeneous local communities (if tolerated at all).[34]

This dynamic of democratic decline would operate without regard to the special economic conditions that created the modern version of democracy—that is, a substantial middle class enjoying unprecedented prosperity due to ecological abundance. The impending loss of that abundance will constitute the climactic disruption of our way of life. In short, democracy as we have known it is entering a perfect storm that threatens to obliterate politics as usual.

To the extent that it is possible to have a strategy for such a storm, it clearly cannot be rational persuasion or the reiteration of scientific facts. (Only about ten percent of the American population is truly "attentive" and therefore even available for persuasion by such means; the situation elsewhere is better, but not by enough to alter the case.) To speak more generally, the problems created by instrumental rationality will not be solved by it, but rather with a vision of a nobler future that appeals to Pascal's reasons of the heart—in other words, by something tantamount to religious conversion.

A viable strategy for change must therefore address our irrational nature, not our limited rationality. Mostly leaving aside

---

34 William H. McNeill, *Polyethnicity an• National Unity in Worl• History* (Toronto, Canada: University of Toronto Press, 1986), and John Stuart Mill, *Consi•erations on Representative Government*, chap. xvi.

47

the established and respectable print media, which reach only the ten percent and have been more or less overtaken by events, those who want to alter the current trajectory toward democratic demise must wage information war in a digital media environment increasingly poisoned by fear, anger, and hatred, not to mention the disinformation and *kompromat* for which it is so perfectly suited. In effect, change makers need to become propagandists themselves, but for a vision of a saner and more humane future. How to go for heart and gut without abandoning reason or stooping to lies and deception is the riddle they must solve. And it must be solved or chance and duress will dictate a future that no one wants.

5.

DISRUPTION

Since its origins, capitalism has been synonymous with Schumpeter's "gale of creative destruction." The gale has now morphed into a hurricane that is genuinely creative but also extremely destructive. Those responsible for generating the hurricane seem almost to delight in disruption for its own sake, an ethos epitomized by the motto of Facebook's founder: "Move fast and break things." But disruption is bound to create both winners who reap the gains and losers who pay the costs.

Joe and Mary Smith live in Akron, Ohio. Joe once had a well-paid factory job that afforded the Smith family a solidly middle-class existence. Then the tire plant moved to Mexico, and Joe has not been able to find steady work ever since, much less work at comparable wages. And with his job Joe lost not only good wages but also his sense of self worth and even much of his social life, which revolved around his work mates. Mary was a stay-at-home mom who worked occasionally for pin money but no longer does so because recent migrants now do all the jobs that casual laborers used to do. Joe and Mary live on welfare.

Joe and Mary had two children. The son, seeing no future in Akron, joined the Army hoping to receive technical training that would qualify him for civilian work after he completed his service. He was channelled into the infantry instead and came home from Iraq in a body bag. The daughter, also seeing no future in Akron, started running with a bad crowd and became terminally addicted to opioids, but not before producing a brain-damaged child that Joe and Mary are raising on food stamps.

Joe's younger brother Pete is still making a go of it as a baker whose specialty is wedding cakes. Pete is a devout evangelical Christian who believes that the Bible is the literal word of God, so when he was approached by a gay couple wanting a cake for their impending wedding he politely declined. He is now being sued by the ACLU and condemned in the national media as a bigot for adhering to his sincere religious beliefs. Pete's daughters attend the local high school where two boys have recently decided to be girls and are demanding to use the bathrooms and changing rooms appropriate for their new "gender." The school is in turmoil and threatened with lawsuits no matter what it does.

Then the black community decided to make its grievances known by marching on city hall under the banners of "Black Lives Matter" and "White Privilege," slogans that seem to mock Joe, Mary, and indeed all those afflicted by disruption who feel that their lives don't seem to matter much to anyone and that far from being privileged they have been thrown to the wolves by:

Wall Street, which sent Joe's job to Mexico and has vastly enriched itself by fostering globalization, digitalization, automation, and a climate in which only the short-term bottom line matters, community be damned;

Silicon Valley, which inflicts enormous disruption on the society while ignoring the costs imposed on individuals and governments and creating a society that threatens to leave large numbers of people out in the cognitive cold;

The meritocrats who believe that they deserve their status and wealth because they have earned it, whereas (at least by implication) those who have not earned it are undeserving;

The corporate hirelings in Washington who have enabled the disruption by doing Wall Street and Silicon Valley's bidding, thereby acquiescing in the steady impoverishment of the American heartland, the gradual marginalization of those who do not qualify to join the "cognitive elite," and therefore the rapid and almost unprecedented growth of stark economic inequality;

The United States Congress, guilty of dereliction of duty for not doing something to control illegal immigration in the first place and then doing nothing to moderate its impact after the fact;

The medical-pharmaceutical complex for its complicity in fomenting a devastating opioid epidemic;

The politicians on the left who (with some honorable exceptions) mostly pander to narrow minority interests instead of standing up for the little guy, the traditional mission of the left;

The national media that mostly celebrates the doings, beliefs, and attitudes of the so-called coastal elites and either ignores what goes on in "flyover country" or condemns its doings, beliefs, and attitudes (however sincerely and deeply held) as backward if not bigoted;

The culture warriors who not only espouse libertarian, secular ideals and mores that are in conflict with traditional values, especially deeply held religious values, but who also demand that these same ideals and mores shall be imposed on all;

The practitioners of identity politics who, whatever their original intentions and motives, have created a climate in which personal identity, personal rights, and personal grievances are paramount, thus negating a sense of common citizenship and provoking conflict among identity groups.[35]

So who unleashed the forces of reaction? Those who believed (with good cause) that their livelihoods and beliefs were under attack and therefore marked their ballot for President Trump? Or those who, all the while congratulating themselves on their enlightenment and compassion, failed to notice the sufferings of their fellow countrymen until the morning after the election?

How the United States arrived at this juncture is complicated. The intrinsic and inexorable dynamic of capitalism that engenders creative destruction, the exceptional disruption caused by the computer and the internet, the implacable logic of liberal-democratic values that incite ever greater demands for "freedom" by ever smaller minorities feeling oppressed by society's norms, and the ruthless way in which instrumental rationality corrodes every system of belief are some of the salient factors. However, one consequence of all of the above has been

---

35 What is worse, the rise of identity politics has encouraged the revival of a white supremacy movement that was largely dormant during earlier times of shared prosperity. To say this is not to condone racism in any form—much less to create a false moral equivalence between, say, the NAACP and the KKK—only to point out the political hazard that accompanies a forceful assertion of identity.

especially destructive: the loss of an establishment or, to give it its proper name, a patrician class.

The words *patrician* and *patriarchy* should not be confused or conflated. Despite their common derivation from the Latin and Greek words for *father*, only patriarchy specifically denotes male rule. Whereas there is no reason in principle that a patrician class could not be mixed gender or even matriarchal, and history provides examples of a female sovereign dominating a patrician class, with Elizabeth I of England and Catherine the Great of Russia being only the most noteworthy.

Patrician classes have taken many forms throughout history.[36] However, in all cases, their function is,

First, to uphold society by observing its mores and modeling its norms (making all due allowance for the inevitable hypocrisy involved), thus giving the populace something to look up to and be guided by;

Second, to direct the affairs of the society for the general good even though this will inevitably further entrench their own wealth, status, and power.

What distinguishes a genuine patrician class from a mere oligarchy concerned only with feathering its own nest is a spirit of noblesse oblige— the duty of those in a privileged position to behave with responsibility and generosity toward those who

---

36 The Wikipedia article "Patrician (Post-Roman Europe)" gives some idea of their variety.

are less privileged, if only out of a due regard for their own enlightened self-interest. Noblesse oblige constitutes the glue that holds a well-functioning civil society together and causes a people to take their cues from above instead of below. When ordinary citizens are respected and well-treated instead of disregarded, they will be inclined to follow the lead of their so-called elders and betters. But when their dignity is injured or their vital interests are trampled by those above, they will withdraw their allegiance, causing the society to break down.

Until overthrown by the combination of an antinomian social revolution in the 60s and the blundering of the so-called best and brightest in Vietnam, the United States had a patrician class of long-standing. Its record was mixed, as is true of all such classes. It originally countenanced both slavery and genocide, failed to prevent a brutal civil war, allowed the excesses of the gilded age, and so forth. In addition, although not completely closed—for example, the second generation of robber barons soon became patricians—it practiced systematic exclusion and discrimination. Yet that same class produced reformers like the two Roosevelts as well as numerous others whose lives were spent in public service at all levels of the society. And whatever their faults and failings, the American patricians consistently set a standard that was followed by the rest of the society.

The current absence of a patrician class has produced precisely the anarchic vacuum presaged in William Butler Yeats's "The Second Coming":

> Things fall apart; the centre cannot hold;
>
> . . . .
>
> The best lack all conviction, while the worst
> Are full of passionate intensity.

Without a patrician center, there are no standards, and so people increasingly go their own ways or take their cues from below, not above. And the society breaks down into fractions that passionately pursue their partial interest at the expense of the larger whole. Hence the moral confusion and political dysfunction that now afflicts the United States.

All of history testifies that in complex societies there must be a stable and experienced ruling class of some sort, for the alternative is chaos and anarchy, whether due to a lack of governance or to a takeover of society by ideological fanatics. The choice is between a relatively public-spirited establishment or a corrupt nomenklatura that regards only its own interests. Our current meritocratic elite is an unfortunate example of the latter, for it appears to have little sympathy or concern for those who have not "made it." Merit is, of course, essential to the operation of any complex society, but when merit overrides all other considerations it entails oppression. As mentioned above, the problem with a mere meritocracy is that its members feel entitled without also feeling a countervailing sense of responsibility. Hence its members manifest privilege in the worst sense of the word, thinking that they owe nothing to the lesser beings who are simply getting their just deserts for not being driven enough or clever enough to join the meritorious elite. In the end, as described by Michael Young many years ago, a meritocracy tends toward a state of permanent privilege that over time solidifies into a quasi-genetic hereditary aristocracy.

At this point, one can only hope that the American meritocrats soon come to understand that it is not enough to give away huge sums of money and that they must instead transform themselves into a genuine elite, into a patrician class capable of leading and governing for the benefit of all. If they fail in this regard, then we may anticipate some very rough beasts, their hour come round at last, slouching toward Washington.

6.

REQUIEM FOR DEMOCRACY

No matter how well founded, political regimes are imperma-
nent because they contain inherent flaws and contradictions
that conspire to bring about their downfall in the long run. The
corollary is that human beings are born chiselers looking out
for Number One, and unless constrained by civil society they
will exploit these flaws and contradictions to their own selfish
ends. In effect, political regimes are subject to entropy. As their
original élan and virtue leach away, regimes rot and corrupt.
They are less and less able to govern effectively and ultimately
lose their legitimacy. Sooner or later, they are succeeded by a
new regime animated by a different political ideal. This is the
eternal cycle of regimes—repeatedly observed, *mutatis mutan•is,*
since ancient times.

Recent events suggest that the almost 250-year old democratic era is now ending in an emerging chaos that is prepar-
ing the ground for tyranny, the regime that classically succeeds
democracy in the cycle. People are all for freedom until until
it provokes insecurity and disorder. Then they begin to long
for security and order at all costs, and this is exactly what the

would-be tyrant(s) seem to offer, often accompanied by promises to restore past greatness or crush ancient enemies.

In "The Perfect Storm," I described how the individual pursuit of more and more freedom has the effect of weakening the civil society that is the indispensable ground for stable governance, especially in a democracy. As in a Greek tragedy, democracy's virtue is also a fatal flaw. For it is in the nature of democratic polity to foster increased freedom, and as freedoms compound they eventually produce an unstable, ungovernable society in which anything goes. The center no longer holds, precipitating a crisis out of which emerges a charismatic leader who restores order, by force if necessary.

In that same essay, I also noted that large, sprawling, diverse, polyglot societies—that is, societies without a fairly homogenous populace bound by shared ties of blood and language—have traditionally been governed authoritatively. In a recent op-ed, Ross Douthat put it this way: "One of the hard truths of human affairs is that diversity and democracy do not go easily together."[37] Why? Because diversity tends to induce insecurity, reduce trust, and reanimate tribalism. Lacking a civil society grounded on shared beliefs and values, it takes an

---

37 "In Search of a Good Emperor," *New York Times*, April 15, 2017. Douthat makes a case for quasi-imperial polity in today's increasingly fragmented world.

imperial polity to unite and rule over all the little communities within a divided society.

These two contradictions—a surfeit of freedom and an excess of diversity—would be enough to explain the impending failure of democratic regimes around the world. But there is also a deeper contradiction within the very nature of democracy itself. This was articulated by Jean-Jacques Rousseau in *The Social Contract*, where he made the crucial distinction between the general will and the will of all. The former is what reasonable and disinterested persons would choose if they regarded only the interests of the community, leaving aside all of their personal concerns and preferences. By contrast, the latter is the mere summation of personal desires, which may be unfriendly or even opposed to the interests of the community. To put it another way, the general will is arrived at by disinterested reason, a sincere attempt to determine the commonweal without regard to the impact on the particular individual. By contrast, the will of all is the mere summation of short-term self-interest at best, or ignorance, passion, and prejudice at worst. Unfortunately, in large and diverse political settings with a wide franchise, the will of all will almost inevitably prevail over the general will. Even public spirited voters would often fail to discern their best interests—"One always wants what is good for oneself, but one does not always see it"[38]—and the many would not even make the attempt. Thus collective decisions in a democracy would tend to be both short-sighted and selfish—for instance, cutting taxes so drastically that government cannot function effectively or spending lavishly on the old while short-changing the young. Democracy was therefore too good for imperfect human beings: "So perfect a government is not for men."[39] Besides, majority rule did not make sense: "It is against natural order that the great number should govern and that the few should be governed."[40]

Warned by ancient history and instructed by Rousseau, as well as by Montesquieu and other theorists, the framers of the American Constitution feared that the ignorance, passion, and prejudice of "the mob" would prevail over reason and forethought, producing a chaotic and dangerous will of all. Alexander Hamilton posed the question as follows in *Federalist Paper* No. 1: "Whether societies of men are really capable or not of establishing good government from reflection and choice, or whether they are forever destined to depend for their political constitutions on accident and force." And the framers were

---

38 *The Social Contract*, II, iii.

39 Idem., III, iv.

40 Ibid. Rousseau believed that democracy was feasible only in rustic social settings—e.g., a group of peasants deciding their simple affairs under an oak tree. Ironically, Rousseau's general will was taken up—or, rather, perverted—by the French revolutionaries who turned it into a justification for majoritarian rule.

certain that democracy would produce the latter: "Democracies have ever been spectacles of turbulence and contention; have ever been found incompatible with personal security or rights of property," said James Madison in *Federalist Paper* No. 10. John Adams echoed the sentiment: "Remember, democracy never lasts long. It soon wastes, exhausts, and murders itself."[41] The framers therefore established a republican regime with a restricted franchise and separated powers. Unfortunately, as is well known, this dispensation lasted only two generations. It was replaced by the democratic regime celebrated by Alexis de Tocqueville, albeit with many caveats about the latent tendencies toward self-destruction that have now become manifest.[42] In short, the greatest fears of the framers with regard to democracy have been realized—and not only in the United States.

To make matters worse, modern democracies face two challenges beyond the ken of premodern theorists like Rousseau. First, democracy has become thoroughly intertwined with economic development. Thomas Hobbes, the theorist who founded modern political thought, made it a prime duty of the "Sovereign" to promote "commodious living" or what we call economic development. Adam Smith and almost all later theo-

---

41 Letter to John Taylor, December 17, 1814.

42 An interesting question is whether the American republic was doomed by the democratic zeitgeist, as Tocqueville clearly believed, or whether it failed because political virtue was equated with property ownership, the inequity of which (too often dependent on inheritance) was almost guaranteed to inspire resentment and envy among the majority.

rists followed in Hobbes's footsteps by making national wealth and popular enrichment the goal of government. Thus political leaders, especially in latter days, began to be judged based on their success in fomenting prosperity, not just filling potholes or enforcing laws. Worse yet, the expectation grew that each generation would enjoy more and better material conditions than the previous one, so the burden on governance has only increased over time. Now that ecological scarcity has begun to bite, however, those lower on the totem pole suffer increasing disappointment and deprivation, and the outlook is increasingly bleak for the entire society. This impending economic failure calls into question the legitimacy of democratic governance itself, not just that of any particular administration. Bluntly put, when democracy no longer delivers the goods, it will be consigned to the dustbin of history by an angry mob.

Putting this point in historical perspective, we are the latest (and probably the last) generation to enjoy the luxuriant fruit of an unprecedented era of ecological abundance marked by a plethora of resources ripe for human exploitation. This abundance is usually attributed to fossil fuels, but they came later. Economic development as we know it started with Europe's conquest of the New World, a bonanza of found wealth.[43] Before the conquest, European societies were politically, eco-

---

43 See Ophuls and Boyan, *Ecology and the Politics of Scarcity Revisited*, 190-192.

nomically, and socially closed. But once flooded by a surge of new energy from the Americas, they began to open and develop. All the philosophies, institutions, and values characteristic of modern life, above all liberal democracy, slowly emerged.[44] Over time, as the New World bonanza was supplemented and then supplanted by fossil fuels, economic and political development proceeded in tandem to transform the world and to create the luxuries and freedoms we enjoy today. With a return of ecological scarcity, however, what abundance has given will be taken away—to what extent and how rapidly remains to be seen, but we can hardly expect liberal democratic institutions fostered by abundance and predicated on abundance to survive in their current form.

Second, contemporary civilization has attained a daunting and costly degree of complexity that has outrun by far the intellectual capacity of a democratic electorate. (We tend to emphasize the monetary and energetic costs of complexity, but its cognitive challenges may weigh more heavily in the long run.) It is not just that a majority of American citizens cannot name the three branches of their own government or find China on

44 John Locke relied explicitly on the cornucopia of the New World to justify his liberal theory of government. See ibid., 191, 204.

a map.[45] In simpler times, popular ignorance was manageable, because the majority were solid citizens with an abundance of common sense and a willingness to defer to their elders and betters on matters beyond their comprehension. (They exercised their political rights primarily at the local level, in town meetings and the like.) Now that many critical public matters require a life of devoted specialization and expertise—in, say, the arcane calculus of mutually assured destruction or the abstruse intricacies of climate modeling—popular ignorance, even if it takes the form of apathy on most occasions, constitutes a threat to the stability and survival of the polity. Elections fueled by passion and prejudice, instead of reason and forethought, are likely to result in ill-conceived policies that increase the risk of war or collapse. Blundering about in complex adaptive systems is a prescription for disaster, and to the extent that the political process has come to embody more emotion and less thought, that is where we are headed.

It is not that educated elites do not do stupid things. They do.[46] Forethought and sagacity have always been in short supply. We are dealing, after all, with imperfect human beings. Yet

---

45 The catastrophic failure of the American educational system at both the elementary and secondary levels needs to be mentioned. Even our vaunted university system is mostly failing in its core mission: teaching students to be more universal—i.e., larger than their petty identity— by grounding them in the full richness of human history and culture. As Thomas Jefferson and the other framers knew, a sound education at every level is the sine qua non of democracy.

46 See "The Perfect Storm."

distilled political wisdom seems to favor a limited-franchise republic as the best compromise between democracy and autocracy and as the best arrangement for the prudent management of public affairs.[47] "In short," said Rousseau, "it is the best and most natural order for the wisest to govern the multitude, as long as it is certain that they govern for its benefit and not for their own."[48] That such an arrangement is unattainable at present goes without saying. Unfortunately, that means we will have to wait until the cycle of regimes runs its course and once again offers conditions that favor rule by a "natural aristocracy" of "virtue and talents."[49]

---

47 See note 42 for why property is probably not a good basis for the franchise. True, the alternative—basing it on competence—raises issues of its own. How is that to be determined? Clearly we do not want to be ruled by a corps of Chinese mandarins or Platonic guardians. (As the late William F. Buckley famously remarked, he would rather be ruled by the first 400 people in the Boston phone book than the Harvard faculty.) Perhaps some combination of intellectual attainment and practical experience?

48 *The Social Contract*, III, v. See also Madison's *Federalist Paper* No. 57 for a similar sentiment.

49 Thomas Jefferson in a letter to John Adams, October 28, 1813, wherein he contrasts natural aristocracy unfavorably with an "artificial aristocracy" of "wealth and birth"—i.e., more or less what we have now.

7.

THE CERTAINTY OF FAILURE

To find a new sense of direction, [we] will need to incorporate the certainty of failure,...[for] if failure is expected, and studied, it need not destroy courage.
— Theodore Zeldin[50]

We are on the cusp of a megacrisis formed by the coincidence of two historical cycles: the lesser geopolitical cycle of war and peace and the greater civilizational cycle of rise and fall. If those who govern us were saints advised by geniuses, and if the populace were eager to embrace change, there might be some possibility of turning this epochal crisis into a grand opportunity to reframe civilization to be both humane and ecological. Unfortunately, it is more likely that events will spin out of control, engendering widespread destruction and chaos. Indeed, we cannot exclude the possibility of a deep collapse entailing the radical impoverishment and simplification of society—in effect, the end of industrial civilization as we know it.

---

50 *An Intimate History of Humanity* (New York, NY: HarperPerennial, 1996), 18.

To elaborate on the the nature of the crisis, the Pax Americana that has sustained world order for over seventy years has moved into a terminal phase. The structure of treaties, alliances, institutions, and understandings undergirding that order has been slowly disintegrating due to profound changes in geopolitical conditions since 1945, most notably the fall of the Soviet Union, the rise of Communist China, and the shattering of the Middle East. Major shifts in both economy and ecology have also radically transformed the world and spawned a host of intractable challenges—such as anthropogenic climate change, which epitomizes the tragedy of the commons. Hence the post-WW II settlement no longer accords with reality. Nor does it still enjoy widespread support. To the contrary, disgruntled masses have recently given complacent elites on both sides of the Atlantic a rude shock, and there may be more in store. What is worse, after decades marked by the absence of major war, the sound of sabers rattling is heard once more.[51]

A two-hundred and fifty year-old industrial civilization is also entering its terminal phase. It is mostly failing to come to grips with the problems occasioned by its success, and it exhibits all of the major contradictions that have driven past civilizations toward decline and fall—ecological stress, overpopulation, resource exhaustion, excessive complexity, loosened morals,

---

51 For more on the cycle of war and peace, see Peter Turchin, *War an• Peace an• War* (New York, NY: Plume, 2007).

burgeoning indebtedness, social strife, blatant corruption, and political dysfunction.[52] As indicated in previous essays, we seem destined to return to something resembling the state of human civilization prior to the fossil-fuel era—that is, to live in solar-agrarian societies in which most of the luxuries and freedoms afforded by an abundance of energy slaves are no longer available.[53]

It is difficult to imagine that such momentous change, tantamount to a collective nervous breakdown, could occur peacefully and incrementally. Indeed, transitions from one age to another in the past have been tumultuous in the extreme. Thus the "calamitous" 14th century described by historian Barbara Tuchman may hold up a mirror to our own future—not as an exact preview of coming attractions, but as a salutary reminder of the anarchy, chaos, and, above all, madness we are likely to experience as the old order breaks down.[54] What Tuchman's work may not reflect is the greater speed and intensity of the process in our case. The breakup of the medieval order began in the early 14th century and lasted until well into the 15th.

---

52 For more on the cycle of civilizations, see my *Immoderate Greatness.*

53 See also "The Shape of a Future Civilization."

54 *A Distant Mirror.*

Our time of troubles will probably be both shorter and more intense, with the suffering proportional to the intensity.

So the question is not whether we will experience turmoil and suffering as the crisis unfolds, only how bad they will be. Which raises the issue of how to respond. Is it reasonable to think that we can steer such an epochal transition to some desired end state? Or will we be doing well just to keep our heads above water and to limit the damage? And given the fear of change and the limits of persuasion outlined in a previous essay, can we hope to convert woodenheaded elites and obdurate masses to a radically new and different world view in time to make a managed transition possible?[55] Given the immensity of the crisis outlined above, and the speed with which it seems destined to unfold, it is far more likely that a cascade of untoward events will be prove to be mostly unmanageable and overwhelmingly destructive. An immoderately great civilization will have its luxuriant overgrowth ruthlessly pruned away; hubris will be followed by nemesis.

In this light, we are obliged to accept the certainty of failure and to lay our plans accordingly. The worst-case scenario is that deep collapse will cause us to fall into a dark age in which the arts and adornments of civilization are partially or totally lost. We therefore need to establish arks, storehouses,

---

55 "The Perfect Storm."

and banks to preserve the knowledge, skills, and materials with which to reconstitute a complex civilization. To be clear, this does not mean providing protected enclaves for a favored few— that would be an exercise in futility, like fortifying the fo'c's'le of a sinking ship. Nor does it mean lessening efforts to forestall or mitigate collapse. To persevere as long as any hope remains is a moral imperative. But we must at the same time acknowledge the extremity of the situation and the limits of our powers. No ship is unsinkable, and long experience has taught prudent mariners to provision lifeboats and practice abandoning ship against the eventuality of shipwreck. We should do no less by bequeathing posterity the tools it will need to erect a new civilization from the ruins of the old.[56]

---

56 See *Immoderate Greatness*, 67-68 and note 12.

8.

GOVERNANCE

If men were angels, no government would be
necessary.
— James Madison, *Federalist Paper* No. 51

Whatever their proximate causes, the grave problems afflicting
humanity in the 21st century are ultimately the result of a lack
of governance. Ergo, the solution to those problems is to be
found in appropriate governance, not in mere treaties between
sovereign nations or in social or technological fixes.

The nation-state system that has been the basis of world
order since early in the 20th century is breaking down.[57] Governments have not been able to meet the challenge of globalization and the information revolution, if only because they have
lost control of taxation—the lifeblood of the state—through tax
evasion and sophisticated methods of tax avoidance enabled
by digitalization and globalization. To put it another way, in-

---

57 States in the modern sense have existed since the Treaty of Westphalia of 1648, but we
can date the existence of *nation*-states to 1918 when the Ottoman and Austro-Hungarian
empires collapsed and national self-determination became a paramount principle of international politics.

dividual nation-states no longer possess the resources to solve their most pressing problems or to fulfill many of their basic responsibilities, much less provide expected benefits to citizens. As their power and authority wane, they are beginning to decompose into their ethnic, religious, ideological, and class components.

The consequence is an emerging world disorder tending toward a Hobbesian state of nature in which life threatens to become "solitary, poor, nasty, brutish, and short"[58] for increasing numbers of people, even those in the richest countries. Statistics that purport to show that humankind has never had it so good are not untrue.[59] However, they ignore not just the reality of ecological overshoot but also the political reality identified by Thomas Hobbes in *Leviathan*: a society cannot long exist in peace without a "Sovereign," a governing entity that lays down and enforces laws designed to keep citizens on their best behavior and working together for the greater good.[60] In short, effective governance. It follows that a globalized society must

---

58 Thomas Hobbes, *Leviathan*, chap. viii.

59 E.g., Steven Pinker, *Enlightenment Now* (New York, NY: Viking, 2018).

60 *Leviathan*, chap. xxx. Hobbes likens the laws made by the Sovereign to "hedges" meant to keep travelers from going astray.

achieve global sovereignty, or it will at some point descend into chaos and war.

Woodrow Wilson was hardly an acolyte of Hobbes, but he (along with others) correctly perceived that a world of nation-states subject to no higher power would tend toward a war of all against all resembling the bloody history of European balance-of-power politics writ large. But the most powerful states (the United States foremost among them) refused to sacrifice their sovereignty to the League of Nations. Hence the Hobbesian dynamic that had produced World War I led inexorably to World War II.

Shocked by the trauma of that war, the victors erected the United Nations and other institutions designed to keep the peace and foment a shared prosperity. But the U. N. enjoyed only the semblance of sovereignty, and whatever moral or political force it once had has eroded away—or, more accurately, has been chiseled away by powerful actors pursuing their national interest. Thus its institutions are mostly arenas for states to posture and pretend without actually doing what is required to deal with the stark realities confronting humanity in the first quarter of the 21st century.

Hobbes is far from alone in seeing the issue of sovereignty as the core problem of politics, both domestic and international. John Locke, the author of the liberal political philosophy undergirding a market society—and, as such, a proponent of personal liberty—nevertheless made strong government indispensable, for nothing else could guarantee both civil and property rights. And with regard to international politics, Hobbes was a student of Thucydides, who identified the vicious circle that has become known as the "Thucydides trap." Impelled by honor, fear, and profit, nations are bound to come into conflict. With no higher power compelling them to settle their differences peacefully, they will sooner or later resort to arms.[61]

Jean-Jacques Rousseau expressed Hobbes's insight with a paradoxical dictum: Man must be "forced to be free."[62] By this he did not mean that men and women ought to be tyrannized, only that they be made obedient to laws upholding the "general will," or common interest, over the "will of all," the mere aggregation of private wills, which inevitably deviates from the common interest. To this end, citizens must sacrifice their particular wills to a sovereign power that instantiates the general will. By making this "social contract" they give up their natural freedom—that is, the liberty to do exactly as they wish—but they achieve the higher state of civil freedom. In Rousseau's words,

---

61 Graham Allison, *Destine• for War* (New York, NY: Houghton Mifflin Harcourt, 2017). See also "History and Human Nature."

62 *On the Social Contract*, I, vii.

"For the impulse of appetite alone is slavery, and obedience to the law one has prescribed for oneself is freedom."[63]

Similarly, avoiding the environmental tragedy of the commons requires what Garrett Hardin called "mutual coercion, mutually agreed upon"[64]—in other words, a social contract to create a sovereign power that will compel persons, communities, and states to respect the laws necessary to regulate the commons and thereby allow humankind to live within ecological limits.

A sovereign power is also necessary to govern a global economy. The logic of capitalism—become rich by internalizing profit and externalizing cost—is the root not only of ecological drawdown and destruction, but also of socioeconomic inequality as well as political corruption when wealth buys influence. Absent a sovereign that enforces fair play, good behavior, and a due regard for the interests of the whole, a capitalist economy turns into a self-perpetuating racket. Similarly, phenomena like the upsurge in international crime facilitated by globalization or the anarchy of the cybersphere all cry out for the kind of

---

63 idem, I, viii.

64 "The Tragedy of the Commons." *Science*, 13 Dec 1968. Vol. 162, Issue 3859, pp. 1243-1248. For a more extended discussion of Hobbes, Rousseau, and Hardin on the necessity for sovereignty, see Ophuls and Boyan, *Ecology an⊘ the Politics of Scarcity Revisite⊘*, 192-202, including boxes 19 and 20.

regulation and control that only a Hobbesian Sovereign can provide.

That sovereignty risks tyranny was well understood by all these thinkers, but they saw no alternative. Juvenal's famous adage *Quis custodiet ipsos custodes?*[65] neatly epitomizes the dilemma, one that was the chief preoccupation of the Constitutional Convention of 1787. Recognizing that the existing Articles of Confederation uniting the American colonies were too weak, the framers struggled to give government enough power to be effective yet limit its capacity to become tyrannical. Even so, it was almost immediately recognized that the new Constitution was too strong, and so it was amended in 1791 to guarantee due process and critical freedoms, such as freedom of speech and religion.

As this example shows, governance has no easy, clear, or final solution. It is instead a perennial conundrum that has to be grappled with over and over. A perfect constitution is an oxymoron, and even the best of constitutions is subject to subversion, perversion, and decay. It will therefore terminate in anarchy or tyranny if nothing is done; jury-rigging the ship of state via court decisions and legislative patches only delays the outcome. Revisiting and remodeling a constitution once a generation—"a little rebellion now and then" was Thomas Jef-

---

65 Who will guard the guards themselves?

ferson's prescription for a healthy polity[66]—is theoretically possible and might prevent the slide into dysfunction. But inertia,
sloth, and a lack of wisdom mean that the historical record is
almost barren of positive examples. Solon had hardly exited the
gate of Athens before his renowned reforms began to unravel.
Perhaps that is why the tacit message of Plato's *Republic*, still
the most probing examination of governance at all levels, is to
abandon the city to its own devices and cultivate wisdom. If
only we had that luxury. We must reconstitute the city of the
world or perish.

---

66 Letter to James Madison, January 30, 1787. Jefferson did in fact urge redrafting the
Constitution every twenty years.

THE POLITICAL

ANIMAL

9.

HISTORY AND HUMAN NATURE

For mankind is ever the same and nothing is lost
out of nature, though everything is altered.
— John Dryden[67]

[Man's] needs and nature are no more changed...
in ten thousand years than the beaks of eagles.
— Robinson Jeffers[68]

One of the most commonly expressed sayings about history is
that it does not repeat, but it does rhyme.[69] So there are no exact
recurrences, because circumstances alter historical cases. Yet
certain phenomena recur with some regularity—for example,
economic booms and busts or the decay of virtue into deca-
dence. Each instance may be particular, but each fits a general
historical pattern, *mutatis mutan♦is*. So history is not random,
not merely James Joyce's "nightmare" or Edward Gibbons's

---

67 "On the Characters in the Canterbury Tales," Preface to *Fables, Ancient an♦ Mo♦ern.*
68 "The Beaks of Eagles."
69 Usually attributed to Mark Twain.

"register of the crimes, follies, and misfortunes of mankind."[70] It has something to teach and is even, to some degree, predictable. Harry Truman put it well: "There is nothing new in the world except the history you do not know."[71] But why does history rhyme?

Voltaire gave a pithy answer: "History never repeats itself, man always does."[72] History recurs because of the unchanging human nature asserted by the poets Dryden and Jeffers. This insight was given its definitive form by the political philosopher and historian Niccolò Machiavelli:

> Wise men say, and not without reason, that whoever wishes to foresee the future must consult the past; for human events ever resemble those of preceding times. This arises from the fact that they are produced by men who have ever been, and ever will be, animated by the same passions, and thus they necessarily have the same results.[73]

What are these passions?

To this question historians have given different responses, but their answers all point in the same direction and tend to

---

70 Joyce, *Ulysses*, chap. 2. Gibbon, *The Decline and Fall of the Roman Empire*, vol. 1, chap. 3.

71 Retrieved at http://www.truman.edu/about/history/our-namesake/truman-quotes/

72 Cited Tuchman, *A Distant Mirror*, xx.

73 *Discourses on the First Ten Books of Titus Livius,,* trans. Christian Detmold (North Charleston, SC: CreateSpace, 2015), III, xlii.

supplement, rather than contradict, each other. Will and Ariel Durant emphasize the power of human instincts: "History repeats itself in the large because ... man is equipped to respond in stereotyped ways to frequently occurring situations and stimuli like hunger, danger, and sex."[74] Driven by their amygdala and limbic system, the seats of instinct and emotion, human beings tend to react rather than reason. They flee pain, pursue pleasure, fall madly in love, leap before looking, lose their heads, become addicted, and so on. To make matters worse, the effects of the passions are amplified by the defects of human cognition, which tend to create an illusion of rationality where none exists. So the generality of humankind—including the average politician—bumbles through life largely unaware of their real motives and mostly incapable of setting aside their passions as they make critical decisions. Those who exhibit some degree of rational self-control or foresight are hailed as saints, sages, and statesmen.

Along the same lines, Ian Morris summarizes the lesson he draws from 15,000 years of human history: "The bottom line is that we are lazy, greedy, and fearful, always looking for easier, more profitable, or safer ways to do things."[75] So Morris and the Durants agree: human beings are the slaves of basic drives causing stereotypical behavior that gets them in trouble or makes

---

74 *The Lessons of History,* 88.
75 *Why the West Rules—For Now,* 194.

situations worse. A particular case in point: financial bubbles are a recurrent phenomenon that are well documented by economic historians and therefore avoidable in theory; yet in practice "irrational exuberance" repeatedly bamboozles the unwary and lures the greedy with results that are utterly predictable.[76]

What Morris adds to the mix is laziness, which causes humans who should know better—a stitch in time saves nine—to postpone and procrastinate, putting off necessary action until a crisis point, when it may be too late. And humans tend to follow the line of least resistance or sink to the level of the least common denominator, because to do better requires more effort and gumption than they can normally muster. Laziness explains why humanity took to fossil fuels with such alacrity in the first place and why it now fiercely resists transitioning to renewable sources of energy. The impending departure of our energy slaves means that our lives will be less comfortable and that we will have to work harder, perhaps much harder, for

---

76 Carmen M. Reinhart and Kenneth S. Rogoff, *This Time Is Different: Eight Centuries of Financial Folly* (Princeton, NJ: Princeton University Press, 2011) is one useful explanation (although economists of the Austrian School might beg to differ). However, perhaps the simplest explanation is that offered by Hyman Minsky: like women who forget how painful it was the last time and decide to get pregnant again, with the passage of time bankers forget the pain of the last contraction and become reckless again.

what we get. So we resist a future in which we may once again have to earn our bread by the sweat of our brow.

For a deeper understanding of the passions that drive human affairs in the large, the greatest teacher is Thucydides. In his history of the Peloponnesian War, he says that Athens and Sparta were impelled by three passions: honor, fear, and profit (sometimes translated as interest or even ambition in the older sense of avidity for power). We have already encountered fear, about which there is little more to be said except that it is often exaggerated or irrational and can be triggered by the most nebulous of causes; thus it arises easily and is difficult to extinguish once arisen.

At the political level profit, interest, and ambition are all variations on the theme of greed, albeit for some larger object like status, power, or empire rather than mere sensual gratification. Unfortunately, the very abstractness of such objects means that final satisfaction is always beyond reach, if only because the fear of loss is ever present: "Uneasy lies the head that wears a crown." So there can be no end to power-seeking until it terminates in madness or corruption. Similarly, the profit motive impels individuals to enrich themselves and to keep enriching themselves until their wealth exceeds all bounds and the society becomes divided into rich and poor.

In the international arena, fear and profit create a vicious circle that impels nations toward conflict. As they jockey for position in a world where "the strong do what they can and the weak suffer what they must"[77] fear is ever present, complacency is impossible, and a good offense seems like the best defense. For Thucydides, peace is therefore a mere armistice in a continuous state of war.

What sets Thucydides apart from the rest is the importance he attaches to honor, which can encompass shame, vengeance, ambition, and other correlates of ego. For the most part, honor is not taken very seriously today, unlike past epochs when it was something paramount to be defended at all costs, even at the cost of one's life. The exceptions that prove the rule today are revealing: prisons and ghettos, places close to a state of nature, where to violate the code or lose respect can mean death; and the military, whose members serve a higher cause and offer up their lives in exchange for the king's shilling. However, political actors—like the warriors in Homer's *Iliad*, albeit in a less flamboyant manner—are also vitally concerned with reputation. It is a rare politician who will admit error, or even that he has changed his position on an issue. And the combatants in

---

77 Strassler, 5.89.

World War I all felt they could not back down without losing credibility, even though they knew that going to war might extinguish the lamps of Europe for at least a generation.[78] "Face" is not a concept for East Asians alone.[79]

To understand the role that honor can play in war and peace, consider the decision of Japan to attack the United States. Sometime during the 1930s, a Japanese general visited Stanford University, and his hosts took him to a football game. Afterward, he turned to an aide and said, "We must never go to war with these people." So the Japanese high command was fully aware that war with the United States was fraught with risk. Shortly before the attack on Pearl Harbor, Admiral Isoroku Yamamoto, its chief author and proponent, told members of the Japanese Cabinet, "In the first six to twelve months of a war with the United States and Great Britain I will run wild and win victory upon victory. But then, if the war continues after that, I have no expectation of success."[80] Precisely six months later, Japan was decisively defeated at the Battle of Midway, a

---

78 The German Kaiser almost immediately regretted ordering the mobilization that precipitated the war, only to be told by his generals that it could no longer be recalled. British Foreign Secretary Sir Edward Grey used the lamps metaphor to express his dismay when he saw Europe lurching toward self-destruction.

79 Donna Hicks, *Dignity: Its Essential Role in Resolving Conflict* (New Haven, CT: Yale University Press, 2013) argues that "dignity violations" are the root cause of the deepest conflicts, whether interpersonal or international, and usually constitute the greatest obstacle to resolving them.

80 Wikiquote, citing Ronald Spector, *Eagle Against the Sun*, 1965.

blow from which it never recovered. If we ask why the Japanese military bet their nations's future on such a risky strategy, the answer is, of course, complicated, but honor played a key role. Roosevelt's policies were designed to strangle Japan's war machine and frustrate its imperial designs, an outcome intolerable to a government run by descendants of samurai. Far better to die a noble death fighting for the Emperor than cravenly yield to the humiliating demands of the Americans.

None of the above gives us a crystal ball. Exactly how the passions will play out in any given situation is never obvious, and there will always be wild cards, acts of god, and other surprises. As recent storms and quakes demonstrate, "civilization exists by geological consent, subject to change without notice."[81] But understanding the role of the passions allows us to make better sense of events in the present and to foresee to some degree the direction in which they are tending.[82] And if we do not like that direction, then we can perhaps change the trajectory by determined action—or, at the very least, avoid actions that will make matters worse or even precipitate war.[83] It is up to us whether peace remains a mere armistice between inevitable wars, whether we tolerate the enormous inequities that

---

81 Will Durant, "What is Civilization?" *Ladies' Home Journal*, January 1946.

82 As I have tried to do in "The Perfect Storm."

83 Some have claimed that Roosevelt's policies were in fact designed to provoke a Japanese attack.

guarantee future turmoil, or whether we cling to our energy slaves rather than make a timely transition to a sophisticated solar economy.

Unfortunately, the meta lesson of history is that, as many have said, nobody seems to learn from it. The most poetic version goes, "If men could learn from history, what lessons it might teach us! But passion and party blind our eyes, and the light which experience gives is a lantern on the stern, which shines only on the waves behind us!"[84] The consequence of this failure to learn its lessons makes human history "mostly the history of stupidity."[85] It may be that civilization is a Greek tragedy writ large: the noble but flawed protagonist exceeds the bounds of reason or morality and pays the price. He cannot act otherwise, because character is destiny. One can only hope that this time he will come to his senses before hubris becomes nemesis.

---

84 Samuel Taylor Coleridge, *Table Talk*, December 18, 1831.

85 Fiona MacDonald, "Stephen Hawking Says Most of Our History Is 'The History of Stupidity,'" *Science Alert*, October 21, 2016.

10.

S O U L   A N D   S H A D O W

The decisive question for man is:
Is he related to something infinite or not?
— Carl G. Jung[86]

The so-called death of God, after which everything is supposedly permitted, has not worked out so well for human societies. Without a relation to the infinite, human beings will tend to lose their bearings. Few have the intellectual and moral resources to construct their own philosophy. The vast majority, cast adrift in a universe without intrinsic meaning, will experience a spiritual vertigo that is the source of countless social ills.[87] If we desire genuine well-being, both individual and social, we must find some way to renew our connection with the infinite. To put it another way, we need to recover our souls.

Existential necessity aside, such a renewal is also required for purely pragmatic reasons. Unchecked by moral imperatives derived from a relation to the infinite, the wolf of appetite runs

---

86 *Memories, Dreams, Reflections,* 325.
87 Ophuls, *Requiem for Mo·ern Politics,* 191-199.

free, with consequences that are more and more devastating to ourselves and the earth. For, said Shakespeare,

> Then every thing includes itself in power,
>
> Power into will, will into appetite;
>
> And appetite, an universal wolf,
>
> So doubly seconded with will and power,
>
> Must make perforce an universal prey,
>
> And last eat up himself.[88]

Worse yet, when people lack intrinsic morality, it will be imposed from without:

> Men are qualified for civil liberty in exact proportion to their disposition to put moral chains on their own appetites. . . . Society cannot exist unless a controlling power upon will and appetite be placed somewhere, and the less of it there is within, the more there must be without. It is ordained in the eternal constitution of things, that men of intemperate minds cannot be free. Their passions forge their fetters.[89]

Ergo, if we do not wish to be devoured or to wear fetters, we must renew our connection with the infinite.

---

88 *Troilus an• Cressi•a,* I, iii.

89 Edmund Burke,"Letter to a Member of the National Assembly," 1791.

How we moderns lost our souls is a long story, but the essence is easily stated. Since the Enlightenment, we have used rational means to pursue rational ends to the end of an ever more rationalized society. But human beings are not purely rational. To the contrary,

> The human is a knot of contradictions and opposing drives: reason and unreason; wisdom and recklessness; faithlessness and mysticism; logic and imagination. We feed on exact science as much as we do on myths, on fictions and fabulations. We can die for others or let them perish in the cold; we can create extraordinary things only to enjoy their utter destruction; human society can be paradise and hell at one and the same time.[90]

Another way to state the point is to say that the human psyche has a shadow containing whatever is not overtly manifested by persona or personality. In particular, the shadow contains what is denied, repressed, or even merely unacknowledged by ego. The shadow is intrinsic to the human psyche and cannot be ignored, escaped, dominated, or eliminated. (Indeed, any attempt to do so leads to the return of the repressed in exact proportion to the force of repression.) When we remain unaware of the

---

90 Costica Bratagan, "Our Delight in Destruction," *New York Times*, March 27, 2017.

shadow's contents, it can become the unconscious driver of our behavior or cause chronic neurotic misery. What is worse, it can erupt and temporarily take over ego with potentially disastrous consequences. But the shadow is not a mere reservoir of disowned darkness. To the contrary, it is also a vital source of energy and creativity, without which we are only half a human. Imagine Shakespeare without the shadow. Thus the way to psychic balance and health is for ego to achieve a reconciliation with shadow by embracing all of the psyche's oppositions and contradictions—good and bad, love and hate, rational and irrational, the whole of what makes us human.

What is true of the individual is also true of societies. The shadow side of our increasingly rational and rationalized culture is a growing irrationality that has no constructive outlet and is therefore likely to take perverse or dangerous forms, both socially and politically. The problem with a purely material and rational society is captured by two well-known Biblical sayings: "Man shall not live by bread alone,"[91] and "Where there is no vision, the people perish."[92] In the end, it seems nearly impossible for human beings to exist comfortably and sanely without a guiding myth, without a connection to something larger than

---

91 *Matthew* 4:4, KJV.
92 *Proverbs* 29:18, KJV.

their petty selves, without a story that gives meaning to existence in general and to individual existence in particular.[93]

This older understanding of the critical importance of myth—a supposed chimera banished by the Enlightenment—has been reinforced by modern neuroscience and psychology, which have rendered the phrase *rational being* an oxymoron. The human mind is a trickster that operates behind the scenes to produce an illusion of reality and rationality. And our ideas are not really our own. We do not construct meaning or opinion, we receive them from the collective—that is, from outside ourselves in the form of myths, religions, or philosophies at the higher spiritual level and scientific findings, political doctrines, or internet memes at the more mundane level.[94]

Thus, although Jung was no friend of organized religion, he sided with Dostoyevsky's Grand Inquisitor in thinking that for some time to come "the vast majority needs authority, guidance, law"[95] in a concrete institutional form:

> Collective identities are crutches for the lame, shields for the timid, beds for the lazy, nurseries for the irresponsible; but they are equally shelters for the poor and weak, a home port for the ship-

93 This paragraph and the preceding one are an abbreviation of the argument I have made at greater length in chap. 6 of *Requiem for Modern Politics* and chap. 4 of *Plato's Revenge*.

94 For a brief elaboration, see Philip Fernbach and Steven Sloman, "Why We Believe Obvious Untruths," *New York Times*, March 3, 2017.

95 *Two Essays*, 239.

wrecked, the bosom of a family for orphans, a land of promise for disillusioned vagrants and weary pilgrims, a herd and a safe fold for lost sheep, and a mother providing nourishment and growth. It is therefore wrong to regard this intermediary stage as a trap; on the contrary, for a long time to come it will represent the only possible form of existence for the individual.[96]

A rational society will naturally reject this prescription and continue seeking solutions to its problems by rational means. But the gap between infinite human desires and finite biological resources is at root a moral problem—How and where shall we place a controlling power on human will and appetite?—not something that can be bridged by merely technical or material measures. Hence the solution must be spiritual or religious lest it be nakedly political.

Many will balk at this bald statement, believing along with the Enlightenment *philosophes* that religion has no place in the political realm. But in fact we do have a guiding myth of eternal progress through technological prowess and a tacit religion in the form of a secular ideology tantamount to a religion—namely, an absolute faith in the efficacy of instrumental rationality.

96 *Memories, Dreams, Reflections*, 342-343. Jung was perhaps remiss in not mentioning that collective identities can also be hotbeds of fanaticism.

The problem is that this "faith" lacks a moral core—in other words, anything that would moderate human self-seeking or the insatiable quest for more wealth and power. Its credo is that humankind must use rational means to become the master and possessor of nature and then use that power to achieve personal and national wealth. The overly rationalized and morally unrestrained world in which we find ourselves was created by this quasi-religion and cannot be reformed with more of the same, only by metanoia. That is, by a conversion to a radically different metaphysical stance that restores humanity's relation to the infinite and provides guidance and practical support for living well on the earth without devouring it.

That such a profound change of collective consciousness will not occur anytime soon should be obvious. History suggests that it takes a prolonged period of more or less intense suffering before people let go of an old paradigm and embrace a new one. To put it another way, soul change happens only after we have received a profound shock or reached the end of our tether—that is, during a crisis in which the old verities and rules no longer apply but the new ones are not yet in place. Such an interim between two ages is likely to be dominated by the human shadow—to be a time of troubles in which distrust, denial, anger, polarization, tribalism, violence, and a host of other evils flourish.[97] This suffering is a necessary crucible for the forging of a new era, for the making of a new collective soul.

It would not be useful to speculate on the form that a future religiosity might take, but I will venture an opinion on what form it will *not* take. First, my own utopian vision—"a more experienced and wiser savage" living in a "Bali with electronics"[98]—is just that: a utopia. However useful as a thought experiment, any attempt to rationally construct a better future disregards the messy way in which history has been made in the past and will almost certainly be made in the future.[99] Second, I doubt that the new spiritual dispensation will take the form of any extant major faith. None of them truly respond to our current predicament and all of them are rooted in a tribal identity harking back to a remote past or fatally encrusted by tradition. In other words, I would expect something new—indeed, radically new—to emerge from the crucible, even if it incorporates elements of the old.

It may be that Hegel was not entirely wrong in seeing human history as a story of progress—not toward a merely rational

---

97 Like the catastrophic 14th century described by Tuchman in *A Distant Mirror*.

98 *Plato's Revenge*, chap. 7.

99 That being said, once the messy transition is over any future civilization will necessarily exhibit certain characteristics—to wit, a smaller and more dispersed population, using far less energy per capita, living close to the land in small communities, and practicing mixed farming and artisanal manufacturing. Thus, as suggested in "The Shape of a Future Civilization," such a civilization will resemble pre-industrial societies socially, economically, and politically.

reason, but rather toward a greater and more expansive aware-ness, a consciousness in which Pascal's "reasons of the heart" predominate and act as a container for instrumental rationality. To put it another way, I believe that social and spiritual evolu-tion may in the long run recapitulate biological evolution, which seems to have greater consciousness as its telos. Thus I would expect (or hope) that a future religion would transcend tribal-ism and take a more cosmic stance, expounding a universalist teaching that offers abundant spiritual succor and moral sup-port without having recourse to the Grand Inquisitor's miracle, mystery, and authority. An inkling of such a teaching is perhaps to be found in the Upanishads or the *Tao Te Ching*.

All this is to take a very long view, but living *sub specie ae-ternitatis* is exactly what is needed now. Crises tend to rob us of everything except ego's immediate fears and needs and to cre-ate a climate of desperation. That is why the shadow flourishes during a time of troubles. Only the long view will save us. For twenty years a Japanese Zen master tirelessly taught retreats, ordained priests, and established centers, not only in the U. S. but also in other parts of the world. Yet when asked how Bud-dhism was faring in the West, he replied, "Ask me in 500 years."

11.

THE FUTURE OF INSANITY

Insanity in individuals is something rare—but in groups, parties, nations, and epochs it is the rule.
— Friedrich Nietzsche[100]

Whom the gods would destroy they first make mad.
— Henry Wadsworth Longfellow[101]

The simplest definition of insanity is, "Extreme foolishness; total folly."[102] At first glance, Nietzsche's dictum seems bizarre: Is extreme foolishness and total folly really the rule in human affairs? Perhaps not everywhere or at all times, but history is indeed marked by madness, and our own age is no exception. In fact, we may the maddest of all. To cite just the latest report from the climate front, we are approaching one or more tipping points that could trigger an inexorable slide into "Hothouse

---

100 *Beyon♦ Goo♦ an♦ Evil,* trans. Helen Zimmern (Radford, VA: Wilder, 2008), 56. Other translations prefer *ma♦ness* to *insanity,* but the import is the same.
101 From "The Masque of Pandora," 1875, but in one form or another it is an ancient adage.
102 *American Heritage Dictionary,* 1975 edition.

Earth," a state utterly incompatible with life as we know it.[103] Yet we are only gesturing at solutions, when what is required is "a deep transformation based on a fundamental reorientation of human values, equity, behavior, institutions, economies, and technologies."[104] If this is not extreme foolishness and total folly, then what is?[105]

However, what Nietzsche had in mind is something more common—namely, an ordinary feature of human history rather than an uncommon development threatening to extinguish the possibility of civilization itself. As Nietzsche did not explain his thinking, we turn to Gustave Le Bon's *The Crowd: A Study of the Popular Mind* (1896) to understand the origin and nature of collective madness. Le Bon is sometimes dismissed as reactionary, but his account, published over two hundred years ago, remains a seminal work on crowd psychology. And he was by no means the first or the last to see the dangers lurking in crowds. As Aristotle said in his *Politics*, "[man] is born with weapons for wisdom and virtue which it is possible to employ entirely for the opposite ends."[106] Hence,"when sundered from law and justice," he can become "the most unholy and savage of animals," a

---

103 Trajectories of the Earth System in the Anthropocene, Will Steffen, Johan Rockström, et al., PNAS August 14, 2018. 115 (33) 8252-8259; https://doi.org/10.1073/pnas.1810141115
104 Ibid.
105 Another folly: mortgaging the future with ever-increasing debt.
106 Aristotle, *Politics*, trans. H. Rackham (Cambridge, MA: Harvard University Press, 1944), I, i.

fact amply borne out by ancient Greek history.[107] Thucydides's gripping account of the civil war in Corcyra would be sufficient by itself to inspire a fear of popular madness.[108] Because Le Bon addresses a perennial problem, he has had an enduring impact both intellectually and politically, as we shall see below.

Le Bon's essential point is that crowds amplify every human defect and manifest new ones of their own. In crowds, said Le Bon, independent minds are submerged in a collective mind that stifles dissent and stirs up emotion at the expense of intellect. Hence crowds are moved by simple ideas, striking images, and repeated slogans that drive out deeper thought. To make matters worse, the anonymity of crowds induces individuals to behave viscerally, discarding both prudence and morality. In addition, because crowds are moved by images that are not logically connected or rooted in fact, members of crowds have a hard time distinguishing between reality and illusion. Thus, said Le Bon,

> Crowds are only powerful for destruction. Their
> rule is always tantamount to a barbarian phase.
> A civilisation involves fixed rules, discipline, a
> passing from the instinctive to the rational state,
> forethought for the future, an elevated degree of

---

107 Ibid.

108 It was their knowledge of this history that led the framers of the American Constitution to establish checks on popular democracy.

culture—all of them conditions that crowds, left to themselves, have invariably shown themselves incapable of realizing.[109]

Freud, Jung, and other depth psychologists elucidated the dynamic underlying Le Bon's description: crowds are subject to "psychic contagion." Unless the irrational forces within the human mind are culturally and socially contained, they can go on a rampage, leading to mass manias, collective delusions, and religious frenzies. "The masses," said Jung, "always incline to herd psychology, hence they are easily stampeded; and to mob psychology, hence their witless brutality and hysterical emotionalism."[110] All of which, said Le Bon, makes crowds ripe for demagogic leadership by "men of action . . . . recruited from the ranks of those morbidly nervous excitable half-deranged persons who are bordering on madness."[111]

If this last brings to mind Adolf Hitler and all the other madmen in the grip of insane ideologies who killed millions of people and inflicted immense suffering on the human race during the 20th century, then Nietzsche and Le Bon are not

---

109 *The Crowd*, xiii.
110 Carl G. Jung, *The Practice of Psychotherapy*, trans. Gerhard Adler and R. F. C. Hull (Princeton, NJ: Princeton University Press, 1985), 6.
111 *The Crowd*, 73.

so easily dismissed.[112] If anything, recent developments, such as television, have rendered them both more cogent and more salient.

All media present an abstract and selective version of reality, but compared to print

> television is not an informative medium at all, but a dramatic one: it transmits images, not ideas; it evokes emotions, not thoughts; and it arouses passion, not deliberation. Indeed, at its worst, it is frankly inflammatory. . . . [At best], because it portrays the world in ever small "bites" of sound and image, television creates what is tantamount to a cartoon of reality.[113]

To make matters worse, this caricature is grossly distorted by commercialism: "The purpose of television is to lure a mass audience with mass entertainment so that mass advertising can promote mass consumption."[114] In effect, television creates the preconditions for an electronic mob exhibiting on a societal or

---

112 For what it is worth, the Wikipedia article on Le Bon contains the following paragraph: George Lachmann Mosse claimed that fascist theories of leadership that emerged during the 1920s owed much to Le Bon's theories of crowd psychology. Adolf Hitler is known to have read The Crowd and in Mein Kampf drew on the propaganda techniques proposed by Le Bon.[46][47] Benito Mussolini also made a careful study of Le Bon.[48] Le Bon also influenced Vladimir Lenin and the Bolsheviks.[49]

113 Ophuls, *Requiem for Modern Politics*, 81-82.

114 Ibid., 82.

even global scale all the defects and dangers of Le Bon's crowd.[115]

These defects and dangers are greatly amplified by the internet, which gives this mob a voice, provides even greater anonymity ("On the internet, nobody knows you're a dog"), and sidelines the gatekeepers who once policed public discourse. Thus the marketplace of ideas has become an epistemological free-for-all—an anarchy—and anarchies rarely do well in the long term.[116]

The ideologues who celebrated the radical openness of the internet reckoned without human nature. Absent sophisticated and responsible gatekeepers, public discourse is subject to Gresham's Law. Bad ideas and information drive out good; saner voices are drowned out by a digital mob of charlatans, schemers, extremists, and trolls disgorging misinformation, disinformation, and venom.[117] Yes, "elite" gatekeepers have biases, blindspots, and axes to grind, but these can usually be kept in check by competing gatekeepers. To expect a good result from throwing the crooked timber of humanity together into

---

115 Many of the issues touched on in this essay are treated at greater length in ibid., chap. 2, 6, and 7.

116 Some governments, China first and foremost, are now beginning to police their national networks, which only means that anarchy will be replaced by despotism.

117 A recent example of mob rule online: enraged Twitterers forced the editor of *The New Yorker* to rescind a controversial invitation. See Bret Stephens, "Now Twitter Edits The New Yorker," *New York Times*, September 4, 2018.

one giant arena, instead of allowing the truest timbers to set standards and make rules, is a kind of madness.

Human beings are herd animals who find it hard to keep their heads when everyone around them is losing theirs. Indeed, to depart too far from what is "normal" risks being judged "crazy." To be sane can therefore mean going against the grain of a society intent on imposing its mindset and mores. Relatively few will even make the attempt, and those who do soon discover that their options are limited or require an inordinate sacrifice. In this way, the accepted madness—in our case, the insane ideology that puts us on a trajectory toward the tipping points—prevails until it brings on the wrath of the gods.

12.

IS THIS THE END OF THE HUMAN RACE?

Specialists without spirit, sensualists without heart; this nullity imagines that it has attained a level of civilization never before achieved.
— Max Weber[118]

Tracing the history of the human race over the past 15,000 years, historian Ian Morris concludes that humanity faces a stark choice between "Singularity" or "Nightfall"—that is, between total technological mastery or utter apocalyptic ruin.[119] In short, between utopia or oblivion, as anticipated half a century ago by Buckminster Fuller.

The path to oblivion is well marked. If a sufficiently large asteroid hits the earth, a remote possibility in the short term, the human race will go the way of the dinosaurs in a mass extinction event. If madmen in charge of nations decide to launch thermonuclear war, unfortunately not such a remote possibility,

118 *The Protestant Ethic an♦ the Spirit of Capitalism*, trans. Talcott Parsons (London, UK: Routledge, 2001), 124, quoting Goethe.
119 *Why the West Rules—For Now.*

a nuclear winter could accomplish roughly the same end. And if current ecological trends are allowed to run their course, a lethal cocktail of pollution, disease, depletion, degradation, and destruction accompanied by economic collapse, social turmoil, and political violence will produce almost the same outcome.

This third path to oblivion is unfortunately not a remote possibility, because humankind has already overshot the carrying capacity of the planet and has so far mostly failed to come to grips with the ecological challenge. It has instead chosen denial or temporizing measures that only postpone the day of reckoning, a grudging response that will burden posterity with a legacy of insuperable problems.

So is salvation to be found in the Singularity touted by Ray Kurzweil and others? Briefly stated, the Singularity denotes an accelerated perfection of artificial intelligence fostering a runway advance in technology that culminates in the emergence of a "superintelligence" far surpassing human intellectual capacities.[120] In effect, a giant computer would run the world and solve its problems better than squabbling, short-sighted human beings.

But is this vision of technological perfection achievable in practice given the constraints of physical laws and biological realities—for example the Laws of Thermodynamics and the Law

---

120   The Wikipedia entry "Technological singularity" provides a useful overview.

of the Minimum? Or is it just the ultimate hubris of technological man, to be swiftly followed by the ultimate nemesis? More important, would it constitute a genuine utopia?

If we assume that the Singularity is indeed feasible, carbon-based human beings would become parasites on what would be tantamount to a silicon-based life form, and it is not clear that a digital overlord would suffer us to live as such. It seems at least possible that it would regard us as vermin to be exterminated as expeditiously as possible. But for the sake of argument, let us assume that the Singularity works perfectly and that it actively supports our existence by definitively solving what John Maynard Keynes called the "economic problem."[121]

Seventy years before Kurzweil, Keynes foresaw technological advances and economic growth such that by 2030 we would exit "the tunnel of economic necessity" and attain a state of abundance allowing us to become ladies and gentlemen of leisure. We shall, said Keynes, be able to abandon the "foul" values and means of economic man and instead "honour those who can teach us how to pluck the hour and the day virtuously and well, the delightful people who are capable of taking direct

---

121 "Economic Possibilities for our Grandchildren (1930)," in *Essays in Persuasion.*

enjoyment in things, the lilies of the field who toil not, neither do they spin."

There are two problems with Keynes's vision. First, we have attained a level of material abundance approximately double the eight-fold increase posited by him as more than sufficient for economic nirvana. Yet we have by no means exited the tunnel of necessity, because economic growth seems inevitably to produce more mouths, more wants, and, above all, more complexity. So the tunnel continuously extends itself before us. In fact, thanks to diminishing returns and an inexorable increase in the cost of complexity, we find ourselves running harder to stay in the same place.[122] Thus growth is a flawed and self-defeating strategy for achieving economic nirvana.[123]

The second concern was anticipated by Keynes: "If the economic problem is solved, mankind will be deprived of its traditional purpose." And this was no small matter: "I think with dread of the readjustment of the habits and instincts of the ordinary man, bred into him for countless generations, which he may be asked to discard within a few decades." Only the uncommon few "who can keep alive, and cultivate into a fuller

---

122 The *estruction* of leisure by economic development was described in Staffan B. Linder's prescient *The Harrie* Leisure Class, published in 1969.

123 This was also the root fallacy of Marxism: that the abolition of material scarcity would necessarily produce a benign transformation of social and political relations.

perfection, the art of life itself . . . will be able to enjoy the abundance when it comes." Hence

> there is no country and no people, I think, who can look forward to the age of leisure and of abundance without a dread. For we have been trained too long to strive and not to enjoy. It is a fearful problem for the ordinary person, with no special talents, to occupy himself, especially if he no longer has roots in the soil or in custom or in the beloved conventions of a traditional society.

To drive home his point, Keynes noted that the existing leisure class of his time had "failed disastrously" to solve the problem of leisure: "To judge from the behaviour and the achievements of the wealthy classes today in any quarter of the world, the outlook is very depressing!"

Making all due allowance for an element of condescension in Keynes's judgment, experience has shown that he was right to be concerned. Conspicuous consumption among the super wealthy has reached new heights—mega yachts approaching the size of destroyers—that would surely deepen his depression. And the "ordinary person" without special talents or deep roots has also largely fulfilled his worst fears. Merely having a roof over one's head, food on the table, and some spending money is not enough. As the proverb has it, the devil finds work for idle hands. "Liberated" from responsibility, career, meaning, and purpose, a significant minority in industrial societies has already lapsed into deviance, addiction, and violence. People who spend generation after generation on the dole in urban ghettos and rural slums or indigenous peoples huddling in reservations deprived of their traditional life do not typically become philosophers, artists, or model citizens. They take to drink or some other means of dulling the pain of existence without a meaningful life. So we are richer than Keynes thought necessary but nowhere nearer economic or social nirvana. To the contrary, dysfunction—manifested as crime, addiction, suicide, and the like—has only increased since his time, with consequences that have begun to impact politics.

The solution to the "economic problem" is not economic, it is social and political. Simply continuing to stoke the furnace of human greed is a dead end. We need a radically different, post-Hobbesian conception of the good life, one in which politics is grounded on some higher value, some standard of virtue more elevated than the satisfaction of desire. As noted in "Requiem for Democracy," Thomas Hobbes became the author of modern political economy by abandoning virtue as the purpose of politics and making economic development into the end of government. What is now required is a more spiritual end.

In practical terms, we must somehow rediscover how to be content with little, like our Stone-Age ancestors. Of course, the conditions that allowed humanity to experience what anthropologist James Suzman calls "affluence without abundance" can never be recreated, nor would we want to.[124] But the "Zen road" taken by hunter-gatherers to the "primitive affluence" of the "original affluent society" nevertheless has something to teach us.[125]

First, enjoying satisfaction and security in life seems not to depend on material abundance. Although practically destitute by contemporary standards, hunter-gatherers experienced their environment as full of everything they needed, and they possessed in fullness the knowledge and tools needed to find it. Despite cyclical privations, they therefore felt secure and content. The idea that they should aspire to more seems never to have entered their heads.

Second, they practiced a radical egalitarianism that restrained individuals from pursuing wealth and power or even flaunting their superiority. Thus a successful hunter, no matter

---

124 Suzman, 256. See also John Lanchester, "The Case Against Civilization: Did our hunter-gatherer ancestors have it better?" *The New Yorker*, September 18, 2017, which reviews Suzman in the context of Scott's *Against the Grain*. Scott is a political anthropologist who has made it his life's work to critique complex civilizations as instruments of oppression.
125 Marshall Sahlins, *Stone-Age Economics* (Chicago, IL: Aldine-Atherton, 1970).

how scrupulously he shared his kill and avoided any show of pride, could expect to be cut down to size by the recipients of his largesse. This passion for equality—or, to put it the other way round, a hatred of inequity—is a phenomenon with very deep roots in human (and even primate) history, and Suzman believes it constitutes a "fundamental obstacle" to achieving Keynes's utopian vision:

> For the hunter-gatherer model of primitive affluence was not simply based on their having few needs easily satisfied; it also depended on no one being substantially richer or more powerful than anyone else. If this kind of egalitarianism is a precondition for us to embrace a post-labor world, then I suspect it may prove to be a very hard nut to crack.[126]

Third, our primal ancestors were materially poor but culturally rich. Apart from some simple adornments and a few musical instruments, they possessed only a tool kit for hunting, gathering, and cooking that was easily carried with them on their peregrinations. Sticking to the bare necessities meant that they were not burdened with possessions and could readily go where resources were abundant. That abundance left them with plen-

---

126 Suzman, 256.

ty of free time, which they devoted to culture in the form of a large repertoire of song, dance, and, above all, stories. And to human relationships: they enjoyed an intense social life within their own band, as well as looser ties to a wider circle of trading and gifting partners.

Finally, perhaps most important, our Stone-Age ancestors enjoyed a profound empathy with creation, a deep connection with the land they inhabited and with the other beings peopling it. And they used various rituals and techniques to maintain and deepen that connection, which facilitated their success, fostered their contentment, and nourished their souls.

Both Nightfall and Singularity lead to the end of the human race—the first to biological extinction, the second to virtual extinction as idle parasites of the Singularity. There is still time to choose a different end: a frugal but decent solar-agrarian economy that has a limited, semi-artisanal industrial sector dedicated to providing certain modern conveniences in a sustainable fashion. Such a society would have the shape of pre-industrial societies and be organized and governed accordingly. That is, it would be hierarchical and conventional, so individuals would have to find their freedom within the bounds set by society, not by standing apart from it.[127]

This would be no utopia. Far from it. We would suffer all the joys and sorrows that humanity has experienced since the beginning of time. But we would still be recognizably human, and we would retain the capacity for a deep connection with creation, a connection that constitutes the true source of lasting satisfaction. For although we now live in cities, our hearts remain primal and will wither without a relation to the infinite.[128] To put it in the terms that Max Weber made famous, the only real hope of escaping the "iron cage" of a civilization grown too great, too complex, and too avaricious is the reenchantment of the world.

---

127 See "The Shape of a Future Civilization," as well as my *Plato's Revenge*, chap. 7, which proposes "Bali with electronics" as one possible model.

128 See Carl Jung's "The decisive question for man is: Is he related to something infinite or not?" which was the topic of "Soul and Shadow."

THE FUTURE

13.

THE SHAPE OF A FUTURE CIVILIZATION

All fixed, fast-frozen relations, with their train of
ancient and venerable prejudices and opinions,
are swept away. . . . All that is solid melts into air.
— *The Manifesto of the Communist Party*, 1848

To navigate through the chaos that will follow the breakdown
of an overgrown, overstretched industrial civilization, we need
a clear idea of where we want to arrive. And we must pick this
destination not solely according to our desires, but rather with
a ruthless regard to what might actually be possible once fossil fuels and other low-entropy resources approach exhaustion.
For it is the energy subsidy afforded by these resources that has
allowed our civilization to reach its current luxurious shape—
one that has enabled more and more people to enjoy unprecedented political rights, social freedoms, and economic benefits
but that has also put us on an unsustainable trajectory toward
ecological ruin. Let me begin by tracing the path by which we
reached our current impasse.

Born on the plains of Africa, we humans walked to the ends of the earth as the original invasive species. No sooner arrived than we fell on the existing fauna, driving much of it to extinction. Although we learned to live and even flourish on what remained, the privations of a hand-to-mouth existence eventually impelled us to invent agriculture. This crude but powerful technology, which turns incoming solar energy into crops, allowed us to feed many more people and to erect civilizations. These civilizations then made it possible to devise even more powerful technologies for the domination and exploitation of nature. Thus, although civilizations have risen and fallen over the millennia, the human capacity to dominate and exploit steadily grew until, finally, we learned how to utilize fossil fuels, a storehouse of concentrated sunlight from the past. This radical boost in available energy allowed an equally radical transformation of human society from agrarian to industrial, from living on limited solar income to consuming solar capital for current needs. This cannot continue. Fossil fuels are finite, and burning them in large amounts creates devastating pollution. In addition, the remaining solar capital is declining in quantity or quality, causing a rapid rise in extraction costs. As in an ancient tragedy, our very greatness conspires against us. We may command more power than ever before, but the basis of that power is dwindling, presaging a steep decline in available energy and with it an end to the industrial age as we know it.

If we now try to imagine the shape of a future civilization, one that has learned to live on a more limited energy budget consisting of multiple streams of solar energy gathered by both simple and sophisticated technological means, then history provides instructive examples in the form of the various pre-industrial societies, societies that were primarily reliant on direct solar energy. From these examples I will try to abstract some common features that suggest the probable outlines of our political, social, and economic future.[129]

All known pre-industrial societies were hierarchies with class systems, usually involving inherited privilege: one person or a relatively few people at the top, a small group of soldiers and councilors serving them just beneath, a somewhat larger group serving that class below them, and so on down to a large bottom layer of serfs and peasants (amplified on occasion by a sub-class of untouchables and pariahs). Thus these societies had the shape of a pyramid, with the great mass of the people at the bottom, a narrow elite at the top, and thin strata of clerks, clerics, artisans, and merchants between them in the middle, with

---

129 For more detail, see Patricia Crone, *Pre-Industrial Societies: Anatomy of the Pre-Modern World* (London, UK: Oneworld, 2015).

the exact composition and shape of the pyramid varying with time and culture.

In general, such societies were quite rigid, even frozen, with little or no social mobility. The few exceptions—the peasant boy who rose to be Pope Sylvester II—only served to prove the rule. People were expected to know their place, defer to their elders and betters, and cleave to ancient custom. Gender roles were fixed: with few exceptions, women were confined to the household, while men dominated the public realm.

Although religious tolerance was common in large empires, conformity with a civic religion as well as participation in shared rites and rituals was usually demanded. In smaller communities, a strict conformity was the norm, and in almost all cases a shared religion was the glue that made pre-industrial societies cohere.

Along the same lines, such societies valued consensus rather than a plurality of views, and their ethos was unrelentingly communal, not individual. To put it another way, dissent was not welcome, and individuals generally found it advisable to blend in rather than stand out. As the Japanese proverb warned, "The nail that sticks up gets hammered down."

Morality too was strict. What was moral or immoral depended on the culture—for example, homosexuality could be suppressed, tolerated, or celebrated—but the rules, written or unwritten, were implacable, and the penalty for transgression was likely to be both swift and harsh. This severity was only partially mitigated by hypocrisy. Behind a facade of probity people sinned in secret, and members of the upper classes often took a laissez-faire approach to morality: "Do as you like provided it doesn't frighten the horses or upset the children."

There were, of course, significant differences in the degree of conformity, rigidity, and severity. Bali's traditional caste system was far more relaxed than that of India, and the gap between Bali and Tokugawa Japan, where a peasant could lose his head for daring to look at a passing samurai, was significant. However, compared to contemporary societies where anything goes and the word *transgressive* is used as a term of praise, all these older societies institutionalized conformity. An individual Balinese might have an equal voice in village affairs, but he had in the end to bend his will to that of the *banjar* or become an outcast.

As might be expected, pre-industrial societies were intensely rural and local, and the great majority lived highly circumscribed lives. This had to do partly with the fact that they were agrarian, and therefore firmly rooted in the soil, and partly with the difficulty and expense of transportation. As a result people were strongly attached to their little country (in the old sense). Rustic values and traditions prevailed, and few traveled far from where they were born. In consequence all but a few critical goods were produced and consumed close to home.

By contrast "the carriage trade" enjoyed luxuries brought from afar, and the life of urban elites was thoroughly cosmopolitain: Londoners listened to Handel and Haydn. Indeed, critics often compare modern times unfavorably with olden times, noting that the cultural level was higher in these aristocratic societies than it tends to be today. As evidence, they cite giants like Shakespeare, Rembrandt, and Beethoven, as well as the architectural splendors that draw hordes of tourists today.

The novels of Jane Austen provide rich insight into the quotidian life of one such society: the essential nature of connections, the emphasis upon reputation, the critical importance of manners and social skills, the awareness of class distinctions at every turn, the masculine ideals of duty and honor, the limited opportunities available to women on the one hand combined with the prospect of social mobility through marrying up on the other, and much more. Austen demonstrates that, however harshly we might judge such a society, a good and humane life was possible under such conditions—provided that one was born in relatively good circumstances, meaning in a society that was not too closed and in a family that had a modicum of property and connections.[130]

For those without such good fortune, life was far less comfortable. An extreme concentration of power and wealth at the top of the pyramid implied an equally extreme burden of impotence and poverty at the bottom. Thus all pre-industrial societies exhibited a strong tendency toward marked inequality of status and wealth, with destitution, peonage, serfdom, and even chattel slavery being regrettably common.

Political tyranny was also an ever-present menace. Despite the existence of formal mechanisms to check and balance untrammeled power, authority could be wielded in ways that were harsh or arbitrary, and common folk often had little recourse against depredation from above.[131] In the end, the core truth of such societies was that the top of the pyramid lived by exploiting and oppressing the bottom.

Some might believe that we will retain the technological capacity to recreate a non-agrarian society, but this is unlikely. Post-industrial societies will be decidedly agrarian, albeit

---

130 For a more masculine perspective on Austen's society, see Patrick O'Brian's acclaimed Aubrey-Maturin series. Although primarily about naval warfare in the Napoleonic age, the novels also chronicle the terrestrial (mis)adventures of the characters to such effect that they constitute a brilliant portrait of English society prior to the Industrial Revolution.

131 Alessandro Manzoni's famous historical novel *The Betrothe* chronicles a predatory noble's sustained assault on the virtue of a peasant girl. Manzoni's vivid description of the plague that afflicted Milan also shows how quickly the veneer of civilization can vanish, leaving behind anarchy and cruelty.

with many technological appurtenances and modern conveniences, because the essential nature of solar energy is that it is dispersed. Hence it will generally be more practical and economical to decentralize production—especially agricultural production—rather than try to mimic the centralized industrial mode of production with more limited post-industrial means. Although artificial intelligence, nanotechnology, robotics, and the like might enable a relatively sophisticated economy based on direct solar energy, the post-industrial economy, like the society and the polity, will probably resemble its pre-industrial predecessors in its basic shape.

I do not offer this brief sketch of the most important elements of pre-industrial societies as a prediction. A future civilization will probably fall somewhere in the middle between those who tout a technological paradise—or hell, depending on your point of view—and those who anticipate a return to the Stone Age. *Although much depends critically on the transition,* we need not revert completely to pre-industrial conditions. We already have technological capacities in agriculture that can lessen farm toil while still producing a surplus sufficient to sustain societies well above the subsistence level. And also possibilities in communication and transportation that can serve to mitigate Marx's idiocy of rural life and permit some degree of liberty and equality as well as some measure of "enlightenment" to persist.[132] Nevertheless, when it can no longer live by expending solar capital and is once again obliged to subsist almost entirely on solar income, the direction toward which a post-industrial civilization will necessarily tend is clear. It will be composed of societies that resemble in important respects those that pre-ceded our age of abnormal abundance and inordinate freedom. If the Industrial Revolution swept away "all fixed, fast-frozen relations, with their train of ancient and venerable prejudices and opinions," then the demise of that revolution portends their return.

---

132 I imagine such a utopian future, which I call "Bali with electronics," in *Plato's Revenge,* chap. 7.

APPENDIX: WARGAMING THE END OF CIVILIZATION

If the litany of warnings cited in the main text proves anything, it is that rational arguments or computer printouts are of quite limited use in persuading officials and executives at any level that they will soon confront a crisis. Nor are they effective preparation for the kinds of challenges they will face once the crisis arrives. In part this is due to the ideology of economic growth itself, which asserts that any ills caused by growth can and should be cured with more of the same, so contradictory information is simply discarded. But another reason is that the ability to comprehend the world systemically in the abstract seems to be quite limited in many human beings. This is not a function of intelligence in the usual sense but rather of an inability to perceive patterns, to synthesize disparate variables into a coherent picture. The reaction to the Club of Rome's original report is a case in point. Leaving aside instances when it was rejected out of hand ("the computer that cried wolf"), most saw only a series of discrete problems that could be solved in isolation, not a global problem that demanded a comprehensive solution. Thus the cogency and gravity of its findings was not always fully appreciated: an interesting report, to be sure, but not something to provoke an agonizing appraisal of one's world view. And the two later updates showing that the situation had grown more dire and the necessity for action more pressing were greeted with collective shrugs.

Whatever the reason for this apparent inability to grasp the world systemically—mental laziness, lack of training, or the trained incapacity of the specialist who knows more and more about less and less—the task is to account for it and to overcome it by communicating both the problem and a possible solution in a different way, one that imparts a bodily experience of the problem and that teaches the utter necessity of advance planning. Since the closest analog to what we are about to experience as a civilization is war, we should employ the military practice of war games, simulations of campaigns and battles that help to prepare leaders for conflict and that allow them to try out tactics and strategies in advance. In this way, they begin to understand in their bones, not just intellectually, what they must do. As noted in the main text, plans may need to be changed on the fly once battle commences, but the experience of simulation and advance planning would at least give those in charge at every level a better chance of navigating the chaos. Now the challenge is to persuade key personnel to participate in wargaming the end of industrial civilization.

LIST OF SOURCES

Brown, Azby, *Just Enough* (North Clarendon, VT: Tuttle, 2012)

Brown, Harrison, *The Challenge of Man's Future* (New York, NY: Viking, 1954)

Carson, Rachel, *Silent Spring* (New York, NY: Houghton-Mifflin, 1962)

Catton, William R., Jr., *Overshoot* (Urbana, IL: University of Illinois Press, 1980)

Cottrell, Fred, *Energy an√ Society* (New York NY: McGraw, 1955)

Durant, Will and Ariel, *The Lessons of History* (New York, NY: Simon & Schuster, 1968)

Fuller, Buckminster, *Utopia or Oblivion* (New York, NY: Penguin, 1972)

Illich, Ivan, *Deschooling Society* (New York, NY: Harper & Row, 1970)

Illich, Ivan, *Tools for Conviviality* (New York, NY: Harper & Row, 1973)

Illich, Ivan, *Energy an√ Equity* (London, UK: Calder & Boyars, 1973)

Illich, Ivan, *Me√ical Nemesis* (New York, NY: Pantheon, 1976)

Jung, Carl G., *Two Essays on Analytical Psychology*, trans. Gerhard Adler and R. F. C. Hull (Princeton, NJ: Princeton University Press, 1972)

Jung, Carl G., *Memories, Dreams, Reflections* (New York, NY: Vintage, 1989)

Keynes, John Maynard, *Essays in Persuasion* (New York, NY: Norton, 1963)

Kuhn, Thomas S., *The Structure of Scientific Revolutions* (Chicago, IL: University of Chicago Press, 1962)

Kurzweil, Ray, *The Singularity Is Near* (New York, NY: Penguin, 2006)

Le Bon, Gustave, *The Crow√* (Mineola, NY: Dover, 2002)

Meadows, Donella et al., *Limits to Growth* (New York, NY: Universe, 1972)

Meadows, Donella et al., *Beyon• the Limits* (White River Junction, VT: Chelsea Green, 1992)

Meadows, Donella et al., *Limits to Growth* (White River Junction, VT: Chelsea Green, 2004)

Morris, Ian, *Why the West Rules—For Now* (New York, NY: Picador, 2011)

Morris, Ian, *Foragers, Farmers, an• Fossil Fuels* (Princeton, NJ: Princeton University Press, 2015)

Ophuls, William, and A. Stephen Boyan, Jr. *Ecology an• the Politics of Scarcity Revisite•* (New York, NY: W. H. Freeman, 1992)

Ophuls, William, *Requiem for Mo•ern Politics* (Boulder, CO: Westview Press, 1997)

Ophuls, William, *Plato's Revenge* (Cambridge, MA: The MIT Press, 2011)

Ophuls, William, *Immo•erate Greatness* (North Charleston, SC: CreateSpace, 2012)

Rousseau, Jean-Jacques, *On the Social Contract*, ed. Roger D. Masters and trans. Judith R. Masters (New York, NY: St. Martins, 1978)

Schumacher, E. F., *Small Is Beautiful* (London, UK: Blond & Briggs, 1973)

Scott, James C., *Against the Grain* (New Haven, CT: Yale University Press, 2017)

Strassler, Robert B., *The Lan•mark Thucy•i•es*, trans. Richard Crawley (New York, NY: Free Press 1996)

Suzman, James, *Affluence Without Abun•ance* (New York, NY: Bloomsbury, 2017)

Tuchman, Barbara W., *The March of Folly* (New York, NY: Ballantine, 1985)

Tuchman, Barbara W., *A Distant Mirror* (New York, NY: Random House, 1987)

Young, Michael, *The Rise of the Meritocracy* (London, UK: Thames & Hudson, 1958)

Wright, Ronald, *A Short History of Progress* (New York, NY: Carroll & Graf, 2005)